THE REFORMATION ESSAYS

of

Dr. ROBERT BARNES

Frewyll can do nothyng but synne.

And all theyr studye , all theyr wyttes, all theyr counfels , all theyr
trafic,and myschefe,with all gloiynges,and lyinges, and with blaf=
phemynge of God,and hys preachers,is nothynge elles,but to kepe
the worde of God vnder,and to withstande that veryte,whiche they
knowe in theyr confcience must nedes go forthe,though all the worlde
wolde fay nay. And therfore wyll they here no man,nor reafon with
any man , but euen fay as Pharo byd, J wyll not let the people go.
But yf they were not indurated,& the very enemyes vnto the veryte,
they wolde at the leſte wayes here theyr poore bretherne of charyte,
and knowe what they coulde fay , and yf they coulde proue theyr
fayinge to be trewe : than,yf they had the loue of the veryte,as they
haue but the ſhadowe,they wolde gyue immortall thankes to God,
and with great mekenes, & with a lowe ſpirite, receyue the heuenly
veryte, and thanke theyr bretherne hartely, that they warned them
of fuche a dampnable waye, nowe in good tyme , and ſeaſon .
But there is no loue to the veryte, nor yet feare of God,
nor regarde to the daunger of theyr foules. And
why ? For they be chyldren of induracion,
and of blalphemy. And therfore the
more it is preached, the more
are they obſtinate.
This is the very induracion, that God worketh in mennes
hertes, wherby they be the chyldren of darkenes .
Therfore let vs pray inſtantly to God, to
molifye our harde hertes , for
Chriſtes dere bloude
fake. Amen.

A page from the first edition of Barnes' *Supplication* printed in
England in 1534. The likeness must be presumed to be that of
Barnes though it has a striking similarity to contemporary woodcuts
of Erasmus.

The Reformation Essays

of

Dr. Robert Barnes

*Chaplain
To Henry VIII*

Edited by NEELAK S. TJERNAGEL

Wipf & Stock
PUBLISHERS
Eugene, Oregon

Wipf and Stock Publishers
199 W 8th Ave, Suite 3
Eugene, OR 97401

The Reformation Essays of Dr. Robert Barnes
Edited by Tjernagel, Neelak S.
Copyright©1963 by Tjernagel, Neelak S.
ISBN 13: 978-1-55635-683-4
ISBN 10: 1-55635-683-8
Publication date 10/19/2007
Previously published by Concordia London, 1963

TABLE OF CONTENTS

PREFACE : BIOGRAPHICAL NOTE . . . 7

I. JUSTIFICATION 20

II. THE CHURCH 37

III. THE OFFICE OF THE KEYS . . . 53

IV. FREE WILL AND ELECTION . . . 62

V. HOLY SCRIPTURE 77

VI. TEMPORAL AND RELIGIOUS AUTHORITY . 81

APPENDIX : Notes on the Published Works of Robert
Barnes 94

A. The Sentences 94

B. The Supplication 96

C. The Lives of the Popes . . . 112

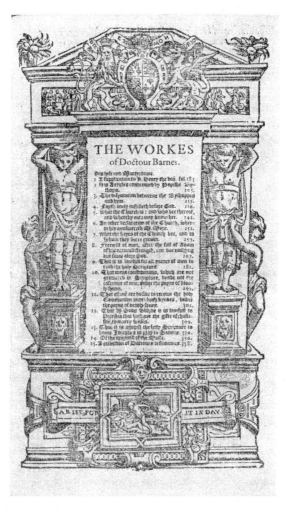

The Table of Contents of the definitive edition of the works of Barnes published by Daye in 1572.

PREFACE

W HEN *The Supplication* of Robert Barnes, printed in
Antwerp, made its appearance in England the brilliant
humanist, Sir Thomas More, read it and said that of
all the books that had come from abroad " there was never
none yet so bad, so foolish, nor so false as his ". The messen-
ger who brought it to England wrote to the King's vice-
gerent, Thomas Cromwell, " Look well upon Dr. Barnes'
book. It is such a piece of work as I have not yet seen any
like it. I think he shall seal it with his blood." A post-script
added : " The common people have never been so much
moved to give credence to any work before this in the English
tongue as they will be by this, because he proves his learning
by Scripture, the doctors, and the Pope's law. If it be true
. . . no prince being ever so mighty can destroy it. If it be
false, God shall both destroy it and the maker of it. Men's
errors in my poor judgment, would henceforth cease if it
would please the king to have this man examined before
himself and the world, thus showing himself seriously to regard
the truth of God's word."

SCHOLAR

Robert Barnes, the author of the doctrinal essays in this
volume, was born at Kings Lynn, Norfolk, in 1495. As early,
possibly, as his tenth year, he was sent to the Augustinian
monastery at Cambridge. This was to be his home until his
thirtieth year. Here he studied, taught, and preached, and
became the leader of that group of men who later were to
be the main agents of the English Reformation. When he
returned from a period of study at the University of Louvain,

his house at Cambridge named him prior, and the University
of Cambridge gave him a D.D. degree.

Under the patronage of Lady Margaret, the grandmother
of Henry VIII, and the leadership of John Fisher, the chancellor of the university, Cambridge had become one of the
most important centres of the new Renaissance learning.
Erasmus, the most brilliant of the humanists in northern
Europe, had taught at Cambridge, and later influenced the
university profoundly through the publication of a new Latin
edition of the New Testament. Many young students read
this volume for purely scholarly reasons and were converted
to the religious views that were emanating from the University
of Wittenberg, where Martin Luther was laying the foundations for the Protestant Reformation.

What this re-discovery of the Bible meant to one of the
Cambridge students of those years is remembered in words
of Thomas Bilney, one of the first converts to Reformation
theology. "At the last I heard speak of Jesus, even then
when the New Testament was first set forth by Erasmus. I
bought it even by the providence of God, as I do now well
understand and perceive. At the first reading (as I well
remember) I chanced upon this sentence of St. Paul (O most
sweet and comfortable sentence to any soul) in Timothy 1, 15,
'It is a true saying, and worthy of all men to be embraced,
that Christ Jesus came into the world to save sinners; of whom
I am the chief and principal'. This one sentence, through
God's instruction and inner working, which I did not then
perceive, did so exhilarate my heart, being before wounded
with the guilt of my sins, and being almost in despair, that
even immediately I seemed unto myself to feel a marvellous
comfort and quietness, insomuch that my bruised bones
leaped for joy."

Bilney converted Robert Barnes and many others who came
to be known as the " Germans " because of their interest in

Lutheran theology. Eventually the group crystallized under the leadership of Robert Barnes and met secretly in the famous White Horse Inn. There were about a hundred Cambridge men of those days who either were participants in the spirited discussions at the White Horse Inn or were directly influenced by the " Germans ". By the end of 1525 they felt strong enough to come out of hiding and chose Barnes to preach a sermon that would make their views public.

It was Christmas Eve and the last Sunday in Advent. Barnes surrendered his pulpit in the Augustinian priory to his friend Hugh Latimer and preached in St. Edward's, the chapel of Clare and Trinity Colleges, where Latimer customarily conducted services. In his own pulpit Barnes was free to speak his own mind because the Augustinian priory was not under university jurisdiction.

When Barnes stepped into Latimer's pulpit (which, incidentally, is still in use) he was confronted by a large assembly, including the university authorities. They had long been disturbed about the new doctrines the young university men were favouring and had been looking for an opportunity to put a stop to the heresies that had infected them. Barnes more than gave them the opportunity they were looking for. He foolishly made a play to the gallery, and, instead of a careful exposition of the Epistle for the day, he launched into an angry diatribe against the clergy in general and against Cardinal Wolsey in particular.

It was all that the Vice-chancellor Natares needed. Barnes was arrested and sent to London for trial. A search was made for heretical books in the rooms of the frequenters of the White Horse Inn. Barnes never saw Cambridge again but he left an indelible mark on a generation of scholars that were to write the most important chapter in the history of the university. Among them were forty men who proceeded to doctoral degrees and over twenty who became bishops. Over twenty followed the path to martyrdom. Many more suffered varying degrees of persecution. Two score of them were exiles on the Continent during the Marian persecutions.

But of even greater importance is the fact that almost all the translators and publishers of the English Bible, Tyndale, Coverdale, Rogers, and a dozen more, were Cambridge scholars in this period. Thomas Cranmer and the men involved in the formulation of the *Book of Common Prayer,* the *Thirty-Nine Articles* and other formularies of faith, liturgy and practice were in one way or another influenced by Robert Barnes. Their activities as preachers and scholars extended into the reign of Elizabeth I and influenced the Acts of Settlement that gave English Protestantism its fundamentally Lutheran character.

HERETIC

Barnes was tried at Westminster by Cardinal Wolsey and several bishops who charged him with certain articles gathered out of his sermon at St. Edwards, of which some were slanderous, some erroneous, some contentious, some seditious, some foolish, and some heretical. No particulars were given him as to which statements in his sermon were offensive. He was simply required to submit to the authority of Cardinal Wolsey and to read a prepared statement admitting his guilt. Up to this point he had been in secret session with the bishops. When, after a personal struggle within himself, Barnes agreed to read the statement, a great audience was brought into the hall to hear his confession. Then he was required to kneel before one of the bishops to receive absolution. The absolution was denied him, however, until he would agree to accept the penance imposed on him. Again he reluctantly agreed.

The next day, 11 February, 1526, Cardinal Wolsey came to St. Paul's cathedral in all his pomp and glory. A scaffold had been erected for him, and thirty-six abbots, mitred priors and bishops were seated about him enthroned with his chaplains and spiritual doctors. John Fisher, Bishop of Rochester and chancellor of Cambridge University, preached a sermon which accused Barnes of heresy and reproved Martin Luther's heretical theology. After the sermon Barnes and five other offenders were required to kneel and to ask forgiveness of God, the Church, and Cardinal Wolsey.

Thereafter, there was a solemn burning of heretical books. Barnes and his fellow prisoners did their penance by carrying lighted faggots thrice around the fire. That done, the convicted heretics were absolved of their sins and received back into the church. An indulgence was proclaimed by Bishop Fisher for all who had witnessed the ceremony. The prisoners were remanded to Fleet prison to await the Cardinal's further pleasure.

Barnes remained at Fleet prison for six months; after which he was committed to the Augustinian priory in London as a free prisoner. During this time he occupied himself in selling Tyndale's English Bibles. When complaints were brought to Cardinal Wolsey, he ordered Barnes to Northampton to be burned. A friend informed Barnes of the writ made out against him and helped him to take flight to the Continent.

At this point in his career Barnes was, by his own later testimony, far from being a Lutheran. Indeed, the charges against him at his trial do not give indication of a specifically Lutheran faith. He had, however, absorbed the interests of sixteenth century humanism and had gone on to a mature scholarship in classical studies. He shared the typical humanistic abhorrence for the pretensions and superficialities of the ecclesiastical order of his time. His relations with the Cam-

bridge "heretics " of the White Horse Inn developed in him
the evangelical spirit of Stafford and Bilney, and the social
and humanitarian consciousness of Latimer.   When he walked
out of gaol in November, 1528, he was a notable example of
English Protestantism.   His development and maturation as a
Lutheran theologian was to take place during his Continental
exile in the next three years.

REFORMER

Barnes left England in November, 1528.   He did not return
until December, 1531, when his first English book provided
the occasion for an audience with Henry VIII.   During his
three years on the Continent Barnes served some months as
assistant to John Aepinus, the pastor of a Lutheran congregation at Hamburg.   From there he went to Wittenberg, where
he enrolled as a student at the University of Wittenberg under
the pseudonym Antonius Anglus.   He spent at least a summer
in the home of John Bugenhagen and was a frequent guest in
Luther's home.   An affectionate relationship also developed
between Barnes and Melanchthon.

Barnes' studies at Wittenberg resulted in the publication
of three scholarly volumes defending and expounding the
Lutheran theology of the University of Wittenberg.   His
major objective was to win Henry VIII and England for the
Lutheran faith.

Between early 1532 and August, 1534, he was back in
Germany where he revised and rewrote some of the theological
essays that had been published in Antwerp in 1531, adding
several new ones.   He was also occupied in the writing of his
Lives of the Popes.   In August, 1534, at the palace at Hamp-
ton Court near London, he was with the delegations from
Luebeck and Hamburg who were discussing theology with

Bekantnus des Glaubens:

Die Robertus Barns / Der Heiligen Schrifft Doctor (jnn Deudschem Lande D. Antonius genent) zu Lunden jnn Engelland gethan hat.

Anno M.D.xl. Am xxx.tag des Monats Julij / Da er zum Fewer one vrteil vnd recht/ vnschuldig vnuerhörter sach / gefurt vnd verbrant worden ist.

Aus der Englischen sprach verdeudscht.

Mit einer Vorrhede D. Martini Luthers.

Wittemberg.
M.D.XL.

The *Confession of Faith* made by Barnes at the stake. This is the title page of the German translation published in Wittenberg immediately after the execution of Barnes. It had a preface written by Martin Luther.

English churchmen with a view to closer relations between England and those Hanseatic states. From that time until his death in 1540 he was in the service of Henry VIII, participating in theological discussions with Continental Lutherans in an effort to create an Anglo-Lutheran alliance.

ROYAL CHAPLAIN

The new role of Robert Barnes was the result of a series of diplomatic reverses. England's alliance with Spain had collapsed. Cardinal Wolsey's attempt to forge an alliance with France had failed. After 1529 Henry VIII and the Emperor Charles V were at sword's points over the question of Henry's divorce. The Schmalkaldic League in Lutheran Germany was the only political power to which Henry could turn in his fear of being isolated in his island kingdom and completely cut off from Continental allies.

Immediately after creating the Schmalkaldic League for the defence of their Lutheran faith, the Lutheran princes invited Henry VIII and England to join them in a Protestant federation. Two factors made Henry most interested in the proposal. The first was his need for a Continental ally. The second was his desire for support in the divorce proceedings against Queen Catherine. The first Continental theologians who visited England, particularly the Hamburg delegation under John Aepinus, enthusiastically justified Henry in his demand for an annulment of his marriage. But the Lutherans at Wittenburg did not support him, though they were far from giving an unequivocal judgment. Barnes, the king's own envoy, was to have the sorry task of bringing the unfavourable response to England. Henry never forgave him his failure to bring a favourable reply.

The effort to bring England and the German princes into a religious and political alliance continued from 1532 until its collapse seven years later. Throughout the negotiations the princes steadfastly insisted that the proposed alliance be based on religious unity and demanded English acceptance of the *Augsburg Confession* of 1530. Henry, a king in his own right, felt that he outranked the Lutheran princes who were the political subordinates of Charles V. For that reason he was reluctant to accept a doctrinal statement which he had no hand in formulating. He, therefore, proposed doctrinal discussions in which English and German theologians might arrive at a new doctrinal formulation that would be acceptable to both Henry and the princes.

Robert Barnes had already summarized the main points of the *Augsburg Confession* in his *Sentences* and in the following years he used all his religious knowledge to secure English acceptance of the Lutheran theology. The first of the Anglo-Lutheran conferences was held in Germany. Its outcome was *The Wittenberg Articles* of 1536. Two years later a conference, held in London, formulated *The Thirteen Articles* of 1538. Neither of these formulations of faith was ever officially recognized in either England or Germany, yet they were immensely important in England because the doctrinal formulations of the reign of Henry VIII were profoundly influenced by them. These were *The Ten Articles of 1536, The Institution of a Christian Man of 1537,* referred to as *The Bishops Book,* and *The Necessary Doctrine* and *Erudition For Any Christian Man of 1543,* usually called *The King's Book.* To these must be added Cromwell's *Injunctions of 1536 and 1538.* These were regulations in the practical aspects of worship and religious life and carried the authority of the king. They were clearly and distinctively Lutheran. When Thomas Cranmer compiled the *Forty-Two Articles of 1549* he borrowed extensively from the *Wittenberg Articles of 1536* and *The Thirteen Articles of 1538*. The *Forty-Two Articles of 1549* were later revised and became the *Thirty-Nine Articles*. Since the reign of Elizabeth I, they have been the official doctrinal formulation of the Church of England.

As the martyrologist John Foxe recognized, Robert Barnes had a far-reaching influence on the development of the Anglican church. His fervent wish that England might become Lutheran was not literally realized. Nevertheless the religion of the English people was to be Lutheran in its essential doctrine and in its liturgical form. The liturgical and doctrinal formulations of the Anglican church were of Cranmer's making. Barnes gave them their Lutheran foundations.

MARTYR

When the Lutheran theologians left England after the conferences of 1538 the work of Robert Barnes was done. The king had never had any fondness for him, and finally prevented Cromwell and Cranmer from getting an ecclesiastical appointment for the English Lutheran reformer. But worse was soon to come. By 1539 the political situation in Europe had so far changed that King Henry no longer needed German allies. The wind of change was apparent when an act of attainder condemned both Thomas Cromwell and Robert Barnes to death without a trial.

Barnes faced his fate calmly and his last words at the stake, a comprehensive confession of faith, were published in Germany with a preface by Martin Luther in which Barnes is referred to as " this holy martyr, St. Robert ".

Luther said, in part :

This Dr. Robert Barnes, who, when with us, in his remarkable humility, would not allow himself to be called Doctor, called himself Antonius; for which he had his reasons. For previously he had been imprisoned in England by the holy bishops, the St. Papists, and had escaped with great difficulty. This Doctor, I say, we knew very well and it is an especial joy to us to hear, that our good pious table companion and guest of our home, has been so graciously called upon by God to shed his blood, for His dear Son's sake, and to become a holy martyr. Thanks, praise and glory be to the Father of our dear Lord Jesus Christ, that He has permitted us to see again, as in the beginning, the times, wherein Christians who have eaten and drunk with us, are taken before our eyes, and from our eyes and sides, to become martyrs, i.e., to go to Heaven and become saints. Twenty years ago, who would have believed that Christ our Lord would be so near us, and, through His precious martyrs and dear saints, would eat and drink and speak and live at our table and home ?

Very soon after the death of Barnes, John Standish (fellow of Whittington College) published *A Little Treatise Against the Protestation of R. Barnes.* The work was an attack on the theology of Barnes' confession of faith made at the stake. The pamphlet came into the hands of Miles Coverdale, who quickly rose to the defence of his former superior at the Austin Friars of Cambridge. He said :

The words of Dr. Barnes, spoken at the hour of his death, and here underwritten, are good, wholesome, according to God's holy Scripture, and not worthy to be evil taken, it shall be evidently seen, when we have laid them to the touchstone, and tried them by God's Word. Dr. Barnes' last will and testament, whereon he taketh his

death is this; that there is no other satisfaction unto the
Father, but the death and passion of Christ only, therefore,
though it had been ten thousand times revoked . . . yet
shall no man's revoking, no, nor your blasting and blowing,
your stamping and staring, your stormy tempests nor winds,
be able to overthrow this truth and testimony of the Holy
Ghost throughout the Scriptures, that the death of Jesus
Christ only doth satisfy and content the Father of heaven,
and maketh the atonement for our sins.   Neither do ye
aught but bark against the moon, so long as ye labour to
diminish the glory of Christ, as though He obtained not
grace for all the sin of the world.

Three years after the death of Barnes, George Joye, erst-
while co-worker of Tyndale, came to the defence of the
theology of Dr. Barnes in an attack on Stephen Gardiner's
articles against the doctrine of justification.   The tract is
titled *George Joye Confuteth Winchester's False Articles*.   In
a prefatory note Joye stated his belief that Barnes and his
two fellows in suffering were burned for preaching " only faith
to justify ".   Gardiner responded in 1545 and Joye filed a
Refutation in 1546.

Thus for six years after the death of " St. Robert," justification by faith continued to be an issue in England, and
Barnes was remembered as its chief exponent.   In the end
Barnes' view was to prevail in Anglican theology; Gardiner's
was to be rejected.

The course of English ecclesiastical history in the reigns of
Edward VI and Mary Tudor from 1547 to 1558 obscured the
memory of Barnes and his work.   During Edward's reign the
influence of Bucer, the Strassburg reformer, overshadowed
that of Barnes.   Queen Mary Tudor placed Barnes' writings
on the English index of prohibited books, but a revival of
interest in his writings in the reign of Elizabeth resulted in

the publication of the definitive edition of Barnes' works in the Daye edition of the *Works of Tyndale, Frith, and Barnes* in 1572.

EDITOR'S NOTE

The essays of Robert Barnes which are included in this selection have been chosen with the purpose of exhibiting the theology of the foremost English Lutheran of the sixteenth century. The last three essays in *The Supplication* have been omitted for the sake of brevity and because their subject matter has somewhat less relevance in the twentieth century than they had when they were written.

All of the essays have been abbreviated in greater or lesser degree. Long quotations from the church fathers have often been omitted. Though all the essays were addressed to Henry VIII, Barnes is often speaking to his principal antagonists, the English bishops. These asides have generally been deleted.

The sixteenth century prose of Robert Barnes has been adapted to the structure and vocabulary of the twentieth century. An effort, however, has been made to retain as far as possible the distinctive cast and flavour of Barnes' style. Bible quotations are in the form of the sixteenth century translation. The original titles of the essays are retained in the subtitles of the selections that follow.

The author gratefully acknowledges the encouragement and counsel of Dr. E. George Pearce and the faithful secretarial assistance of Anna Brue. This little volume is dedicated to the men and women of the Evangelical Lutheran Church of England who are continuing the work of Robert Barnes in the British Isles.

N. S. TJERNAGEL.

Richmond, Surrey.
FEBRUARY 11, 1963.

" *Lord if Thou straightly mark our iniquity, who is able to abide Thy judgment ? Wherefore I trust in no work that ever I did, but only in the death of Jesus Christ. I do not doubt, but through Him to inherit the kingdom of heaven.*"

— Robert Barnes at Smithfield, 30 July, 1540.

I

JUSTIFICATION*

Only Faith Justifieth Before God

IN Holy Scripture Christ is revealed as nothing but a
Saviour, a Redeemer, a Justifier, a perfect Peace-maker
between God and man. This is the testimony the angel
gave in the words: "He shall save his people from their
sins" (Matthew 1, 21). St. Paul says: "Christ is made our
righteousness, our satisfaction, and our redemption" (1
Corinthians 1, 30). The prophet witnesses the same saying:
"For the wretchedness of my people have I stricken him".

Now if we will truly confess Christ, then we must grant
with our hearts that Christ is all our justice, all our redemption, all our wisdom, all our holiness, and alone the purchaser
of grace and the peacemaker between God and man. Briefly
all the goodness that we have is of Him, by Him, and for
His sake alone. We must confess that we have need of
nothing toward our salvation but Him alone and that we
desire no other salvation or help of any other creature either
heavenly or earthly. St. Peter says: "There is no other
name given unto men wherein they must be saved" (Acts
4, 12). St. Paul also says: "By him are all that believe justified from all things" (Acts 13, 39). St. John witnesses the

* *See note on page 102*

same in these words : " He it is that hath obtained grace for our sins " (1 John 2) and, " He sent his son to make agreement for our sins " (1 John 4, 10).

Now here you have Christ in the fulness and wholeness of His nature. He that denies this or any part of these things, or takes any part of them and applies them or gives their glory to any other person than to Christ alone, robs Christ of His honour, denies Him, and is therefore the very Antichrist.

St. Paul says : " All men are sinners and lack the glory of God, but they are justified freely by His grace through the redemption that is in Christ Jesus " (Romans 3, 24). What does it mean that all men have sinned and yet are justified freely ? How shall a sinner do good works ? How can he deserve to be justified ? What is meant by the word freely ? If there is any deserving, either more or less, then it is not received freely. What is meant by grace ? If it be of works then it is not of grace, for then, as St. Paul says : " Grace were not grace " (Romans 11, 6). There can be no evasion because the words are plain. If you submit any works, then by so much is our redemption not freely given. Any part that results from works cannot be of grace. If you bring works for your salvation you have nullified the words of St. Paul because he contends against works and excludes them in justification, bringing grace alone. St. Paul says : " We do judge, therefore, that a man is justified by faith without the works of the law " (Romans 3, 28). Do you not hear that glorying for the sake of works is excluded ? This is Paul's proposition which he sets out to prove, namely, that faith alone justifies. It were a lost labour for him to prove that works help toward justification. That the Jews did grant. They required no more than that works might not be clearly excluded. They were converted and were content to receive Christ as their Saviour, but not only and alone.

It may be said at this point that Paul condemned the works of the old law, but not the works of the new law. But what works can you do or imagine that are not in and of the old law ? Paul speaks of all manner of works, because the law includes all works that God ever instituted. The highest, the best, and the most perfect of all works are the works of the Ten Commandments. These are the works of the old law and they cannot justify. Now what works of the new law, other than these, or better than these, do you have ? Our Master Christ shows that in the fulfilling of these commandments all works are included. What works, then, are in the new law that were not commanded in the old ? Perhaps you will say that all those works that Christ speaks of in the fifth chapter of Matthew are of the new law and not of the old.

To this I answer that our Master Christ there reproves the false interpretation that the Scribes and Pharisees applied to the law. He teaches no new works nor is He the giver of a new law. St. John says : " The law is given through Moses, but grace and truth came by Jesus Christ " (John 1, 17). He is the giver of grace and not another Moses. Therefore to purchase favour for us He died on the cross. This did not Moses. He commanded us to do this and to do that. But Christ says, " Trust in my doing, and believe that I have done this for thee, and not for Myself ".

Christ, I say, interprets and declares the old law against the Scribes and Pharisees who taught that the law was fulfilled with outward works. This false doctrine our Master Christ reproves and says that the law requires a pure and clean heart and will have good works fulfilled out of the heart and not alone with hand and foot, tooth and nail, as the Pharisees say and teach. Thus Christ teaches no new works but only expresses the virtue of the old law.

Moreover, look in the old laws and you shall find that the

words of the law and Christ's exposition do agree. Therefore our Master teaches no new thing nor any new works. But now grant that there are certain works of the new law which are not of the old, you still cannot prove that they shall justify. There can be no more goodness in these works than there were in works of the old law for they were to God's honour and to the profit of our neighbour. What more goodness can works have ? And yet you grant that the old works cannot justify. How then shall your new works justify ? Blessed St. Paul disputes against those who were converted and had works both of the old law and of the new, and yet he concludes that Christ alone was their justifier. Mark his arguments. If righteousness comes of the law then Christ is dead in vain. It is as if he would say that if the law helps to justify (for that was the opinion of the Jews) then Christ is not alone your justifier. If He is not alone your justifier then He died in vain. How will St. Paul prove this conclusion ? In this manner; either Christ does this thing alone, or else He is dead in vain, for He will have no helper. This is the meaning of his arguments.

St. Paul asks you to believe that no manner of good works, though they be as good as Abraham's works, can help toward justification. St. Paul also notes that Abraham was justified many years before the law was given. Therefore, he says, the law does not justify. In the same way I dispute against your new works. Men were sufficiently and perfectly justified by faith alone before any new works were given or preached. Isaiah, Jacob, and John the Baptist and all the holy prophets were perfectly justified before any new works, as you describe them, were spoken of. St. Paul's statement stands firm and strong saying that we are freely and solely justified by faith without any kind of works.

Origin says that " the justification of faith alone is sufficient. If a man believes, he is justified, though no works are done

by him at all. The thief was justified by faith without the
works of the law. Our Lord did not ask him what works
he had done, nor did He demand any works of him, but
accepted him solely for confessing Christ. Therefore it
follows that a man is justified by faith. The works of the
law help nothing." Are these not plain words ? Grant them
and we will ask no more of you.

In the ninth chapter of Romans St. Paul refers to the
Gentiles who knew nothing of God, had done no good works,
but on the contrary had blasphemed God and His name and
had lived in idolatry and had been bitter enemies to all
goodness. Then he speaks of the Jews, full of good works of
the law and of great zeal toward God and to His works. Yet,
with all their good works, St. Paul excludes them from
justification with all their good zeal and all their good works
and says that a Gentile, full of damnable words and possessing
neither zeal or love of goodness, is justified by faith alone.
These are St. Paul's words : " The Gentiles which followed
not righteousness have obtained righteousness, I mean, the
righteousness that cometh of faith. But Israel which followeth
the law of righteousness could not attain unto righteousness.
Why ? Because he sought it not by faith, but, as it were,
by the works of the law " (Romans 9, 31-32). Are not these
words plain ? The Gentiles which followed no righteousness,
nor had any mind toward it, are justified freely by faith.
Is this not faith alone ? Further the Jew is reproved with all
his zeal, with all his love, with all his study, and with all his
good works.

Here it may be said that the good works of the Jews did
not help because they had no faith, and that if they had had
faith, then their works would have helped toward their
justification. To this I answer that it is false to say that
works would have helped if they had had faith. St. Paul
says clearly that good works contribute nothing to salvation,

and evil works do not hinder the justification that comes of faith. No manner of works, whether they are in faith or out of faith can help to justify. Nevertheless works have their glory and reward. But the glory and promise of justification belongs to Christ alone. St. Paul shows plainly in these words that works have no place in justification : " To him that worketh is the reward not given of favour, but of duty. To him that worketh not, but believeth in Him that justifies the wicked man is faith accounted for righteousness " (Romans 4, 4-5). Mark how St. Paul says that righteousness is imputed to him : therefore it is not deserved. That which is deserved is not imputed by favour, but must be given of obligation. Is not this faith alone ? Does St. Paul not clearly exclude works ?

God has decreed that He will require nothing toward justification but faith. He is blessed to whom God imputes justification without works and without all manner of observances. Their sins are covered and no works of penance are required of them; they need only believe.

St. Paul proves the justification of faith alone in these words. He says : " No man is justified by the works of the law, but by the faith of Jesus Christ, and we do believe in Jesus Christ that we may be justified by faith in Christ and not by the works of the law " (Galatians 2, 16). This is also affirmed by the prophet who says : " A righteous man liveth by faith " (Habakkuk 2, 4). What do you call living by faith ? If he lives any part by works, then he does not live by faith, but partly by works. Augustine says that the works that are done before faith, though they seem laudable to men, are but vain. Therefore let no man count his good works before faith Where there is no faith, there is no good work. The intention makes the good work, but faith guides the intention. Mark how the good intention of which you boast is blind and does not know what to do without faith

to guide it. But, when faith comes, it both justifies and
makes those works good which before were sinful.

Now that faith purchases remission of sins is proved by the
article of our faith : " I believe in the forgiveness of sins ".
Why do I need to believe the remission of sins if I may deserve
it by works ? Our Master Christ declares clearly that no
kind of works, whatsoever they are, can justify before God.
These are His words : " When you have done all things that
are commanded you, yet say that we are unprofitable servants " (Luke 17, 10). If you are unprofitable, then you are
not justified. And if you cannot be justified when you have
done all things, how will you be justified ? When, in a
sense, you do nothing, and especially of those things that
are commanded you, then it is plain that our works cannot
help toward justification.

Let us suppose that our noble prince would call all the
bishops before him and say, " My lords, it has pleased us to
call you to the spiritual dignity of bishops, to place you on
our council, and to make you lords of our realm and of our
parliament." Now we would ask which of you have deserved
it or considers himself worthy of it by his own deserving.
What will you say to this ? What will you answer to the
king's grace ? Is there any one among you all that would
be as bold as to say to the king's grace that he had not given
the bishopric to him freely, but that he had done the king
such faithful service that he was bound to give him the
appointment because of his deserving ? If there were one
that were so proud as to say this, do you not think that the
king would lay to his charge that he had not half done his
duty, but were rather bound to do ten times more, and yet
the king's grace were not bound to give him a bishopric, for
he had only done his duty, and not all of that ?

Now if your good works and all your faithful service were
not able to deserve a bishopric of the king's grace, how will

you be able by your works to deserve heaven and justification before the King of all kings ?   When you have answered to this before the king's grace, then come and dispute with God the justification of your works.   Therefore, I conclude by the Scriptures and the doctors that the faith which we have in Christ Jesus and His blessed blood, alone and sufficiently justify us before God, without the help of any works.

The very true way of justification is this.   First comes God, for the love of Christ Jesus, solely by His mercy, and gives us the free gift of faith through which we do believe God and His holy Word and stick fast to the promises of God, and believe that though heaven and earth and all that is in them should perish and come to naught, yet God shall be found true to His promises for this faith's sake if we are the elect children of God.

This is not such a faith as men have when they believe that there is one God, believe that He is eternal, that He made the world of nothing, yes, and believe that the Gospel and all God's words are true and must be fulfilled.   This is not the faith by which we are justified, for devils and infidels have this faith, and we may attain to these things by strength of reason.   But the faith that shall justify us must be another kind of faith for it must come from heaven and not from the strength of reason.   It must make me believe that God the maker of heaven and earth is not only a father, but my Father, and that He has made me His heir through the favour that Christ has purchased me, from which neither heaven nor earth, tribulation or persecution, death nor hell can divide me.   I stick fast to this that He is not only my Father, but also a merciful Father, so merciful that He will not impute my sins unto me though they are ever so great so long as I hold to the blessed blood of Christ Jesus and sin not of malice, but of frailty and of no pleasure.

He is also a liberal Father, so liberal to me that He will

not only promise me all things, but will also give them to
me, whether they are necessary for the body or the soul.
He is not only liberal, but is mighty to perform all things
that He promises me.   Briefly this faith makes me hold to
God and to His blessed promises made in Christ through His
sweet and precious blood.   I do not fear death or any
affliction, persecution or tribulation, but despise all these
things, and not only these, but even my own life, for Christ's
sake.

Finally, I say, of a fleshy beast justification makes me a
spiritual man, of a damnable child it makes me a heavenly
son, of a servant of the devil it makes me a free man of God.
It delivers me from the law, from sin, from death, from the
devil and from all miseries that might hurt me.

This is the faith that justifies.   This is what we preach.
Because it is given from heaven into our hearts by the Spirit
of God it can be no idle thing.   It must do those things that
are to the honour of God and to the profit of our neighbour.
It must do good works, and bring forth the good works that
help and profit men.   But these works are not done to justify
the man, but a justified man must needs do them.   Nor are
they done to his own profit but only to the profit of other
men, even as our Master Christ suffered hunger and thirst
and persecution, taking great labour in preaching the Word.
Finally He also suffered death.   All these things He did, not
to profit Himself, but for our merit and for our profit.   So
likewise a just man does his works : as a good tree in season
brings forth good apples, not to make itself good, because it
is already a good tree, nor are the apples to the profit of the
tree, but rather to the profit of men.   Indeed the good nature
that is in the tree compels it to bring forth good fruit.   So
man must do good works, not to be justified by them, but
only to serve his brother.   He has no need of them for his
own justification.

But now comes fleshly reason and asks, " What need we have to do any good works if we are justified by faith alone ?" Why do we need to crucify or mortify our flesh if these do not profit us and if we shall be saved even though we do no good works ? Thus blind reason disputed with St. Paul when he had proved that God of His mercy had freely delivered us from the damnable bondage of the law. To this he answered, " If we do the works of sin, we are the servants of sin; but if we do works of righteousness, then we are the servants of righteousness. If we truly have the faith that justifies us, we will desire to do no other works than those that belong to justification; not that the works justify, but that we must needs do these works as the true fruit of justification, not its cause." Therefore those who will do no good works because they are justified by faith alone are not the children of God nor the children of justification. If they were the very true children of God, they would be the happier to do good works because they are justified freely. Therefore, should they also freely be moved to works if for no other purpose than to do the will of their merciful God who has so freely justified them, as well as for the profit of their neighbour whom they are bound to serve out of true love.

My Lord of Rochester, Bishop John Fisher, says that faith begins justification in us, but works do perform it and make it perfect. What Christian man would think that a bishop would thus trifle and play with God's holy Word ? Does not St. Paul say that our justification is only of faith and not of works ? If works make justification perfect, then St. Paul's words are not true. St. Paul says we are the children of God by faith. Will you now say that faith merely begins justification ? How can you bring works to make justification perfect when St. Paul has excluded them ?

Another objection, an open falsehood, says that I destroy

all good works and desire that no good works be done, but that a man shall only believe. Tell me a learned person that ever said or taught that men should do no good works. There are many, like St. Paul and all his scholars, who say that good works do not justify, but no one denies good works. I pray you what kind of conclusion is this, according to your own logic ? Works do not justify, therefore we need not do them but may despise them for they are of no value. Take a similar conclusion. You say that the King's grace does not justify, therefore you despise him ? Therefore he is no longer king ? The sun and moon do not justify. Do you therefore destroy them ? St. Paul was opposed by similar logic when he had proved that faith alone justified. Then came your fathers and said that he destroyed the law because he taught that it did not justify. " God forbid," he said, " for we teach the very way to fulfil the law, that is through faith through which alone the law is fulfilled, and without which all the works of the law are but sin. " So we likewise teach the way through which good works are done. First a man is justified by faith, then the just man must needs do works which before were sin, but now are all good, yea his eating, drinking, and sleeping are good.

They use certain Scriptures to prove their point. First they refer to St. James who says : " Wilt thou understand, O thou vain man, that faith without works is dead ? Was not Abraham our father justified by his deeds, when he offered his son Isaiah on the altar ? Likewise, was not Rahab the harlot justified when she received the messengers and sent them out another way ?" (James 2, 20-22). St. Augustine declares in various places that the blessed St. Paul and St. James seemed to disagree in this matter. Therefore St. Augustine, willing to save the estimation of this Epistle said that St. Paul speaks of works that go before faith, and St. James speaks of works that follow faith. Yet St. Augustine

is not compelled by the words of this Epistle to grant that
any works do justify because St. Paul's words are so apparently
and so vehemently to the contrary. Therefore, since there is
a controversy here in two places of Scripture, it stands with
all reason and learning that the place which seems to be the
weakest and the darkest should be expounded and declared
by that part of Scripture that is clearest and of most authority.
Now it is true that the authority of St. Paul has always, in
the church of God, been of higher estimation and strength
than this Epistle of James ever was (though this Epistle has
been received by the church) and especially in the matter
that we speak of here. In all of Scripture this article of
justification is nowhere so plainly and comprehensively treated
as by the blessed St. Paul. This every learned man must
grant. Therefore, it stands with reason and learning that this
saying of James must be reduced and brought to the meaning
of St. Paul, and not St. Paul to the saying of St. James.

Now both St. Paul and St. James mean that good works
should be done, and that they that are Christians should
not be idle and do no good. Because they are the children
of grace, their life should express their outward goodness
received of grace. As St. Paul says, they should " give their
members to be servants unto righteousness as before they were
servants unto uncleanness " (Romans 6, 19). Therefore, the
words of St. James must be understood to be written against
those who, of an idle and vain opinion, boasted of their good
faith. In order to prove that this faith was but an idle thing
and of no effect, St. James demonstrated that it did not bring
forth the appropriate good works. Therefore, he called it
a dead faith. He described a naked brother who had need
of clothing to these men who boasted of their faith and had
no compassion toward his necessity. His conclusion is that
they have no true faith and he says to them, " show me your
faith without works, and I will show you my faith by works."

It is clear that St. James would say no more than that faith without works is dead and has no value. Works should declare and show the outward faith. They should be an external demonstration and testimony of the inner justification that is received through faith. Not that works can or may take away our sin or be the satisfaction for any part of sin, for that is of Christ Jesus. Saints John and Paul say that Christ has appeared once for all to put sin to flight by offering Himself up for us. That this is the meaning of St. James is manifest by what follows : " Thou seest that faith wrought in Abraham's deeds, and through the deeds was his faith made perfect " (James 2, 22).

Mark how faith worked in his deeds. That is, his faith, because it was a living faith brought forth and wrought the high work of oblation. His faith was perfect through his deeds. His faith was manifest and made a great testimony before all the world. The faith that Abraham had was a living and a perfect and a right-sharpen faith. Thus, his inward faith proved him before God, and his outward works done before the world were good and showed that he was justified. In this way, his faith was made perfect before God and man.

Now we do all agree that faith alone justifies before God. In the right time and place this faith does good works and becomes a living thing of God which cannot be dead or idle in man. Yet for all that, we give to faith and to Christ's blood the glory that belongs to them alone, namely justification, the remission of sins, the satisfaction of God's wrath, the taking away of cruel vengeance, the purchasing of mercy, the fulfilling of the law, and all other like things. The glory of these, I say, belongs to Christ only and we are partakers of them through faith in Christ's blood alone. It is no work that receives the promise made in Christ's blood, but faith alone.

The glory and promise of justification belongs only to faith in Christ's blood and not to works of any kind. Nevertheless we do laud and praise good works and diligently teach men to do good works since God has commanded them. We urge them also so that those who blaspheme the truth might be moved by the virtuous life and conversation of Christians to accept the holy religion of Christ.

For these and other reasons I teach good men to live virtuously and well, yes, and also that good works shall have a reward of God, as Scripture testifies, though remission of sins and justification are not the reward referred to. The words of St. James must be held against those who boast of a vain faith that is only an idle opinion and no true faith. His words spoken against a dead faith that does not justify supports me rather than contradicts me.

But you have another Scripture which you cite against me. " Before God they are not justified who hear the law, but they which do the law shall be justified " (Romans 2, 13). You glory in this text and cry, " works, works ! " But if you would consider the mind of St. Paul, you would perceive that he does not speak of works deserving justification. He would not have written in this way against the Jews because they did perform the works of the law to the uttermost, and yet they were not justified. By the hearers of the law, St. Paul means those that do the outward works of the law for fear or for reward, or out of hypocrisy, or to be justified by them. He calls those the doers of the law who do the works of the law according to its intent and as the law commands them, that is in the true faith in Christ Jesus who is the end of the law and the fulfilling of the law, as St. Paul says, to all them that believe. Therefore, men are only hearers of the law until they have the faith of Christ Jesus which is imputed to them for justice. The works of the law can be no cause of justification but only an outward testimony and a witness that the law is fulfilled inwardly in their conscience before God. Christ has made satisfaction for them and they become partakers of it through faith. St. Augustine supports me in saying that none can be " doers of the law except they be first justified, not that justification belongs to doers but that justification precedes all manner of doing."

You also refer to the Gentile, Cornelius, who did great alms and prayed to God steadfastly. The angel said of him : " Thy prayer and thy alms are come into remembrance in the presence of God " (Acts 10, 4). From this text you gather that his good works justified him. To this I answer that the Holy Ghost clearly indicated His presence; therefore, He said that Cornelius was a devout man who feared God. How could this be unless God had taught Cornelius inwardly through faith ? How could he know God, and that devoutly, but by faith ? Therefore, he was justified before God by his faith alone, but the world did not know his justification. Therefore, the Holy Ghost declared his inward justification when he said that he was devout and feared God. He also openly showed the fruits of his justification when he did alms.

You submit in your favour also another Scripture that declares : " If I have all faith so that I may transpose mountains, and have no charity I am nothing " (1 Corinthians 13, 2). From this you gather that faith without charity cannot justify. I answer that you cannot gather this from St. Paul because it is clear that he is not speaking of that by which a man may be justified. He is saying that they who are justified must do works of charity. It is also plain that he does not speak of faith that justifies inwardly, but of the faith that works outwardly. This is called a gift of the Holy Ghost like the gift of tongues, the gift of prophecies, the gift of healing, and the gift of interpretation, as is clear from the previous chapter. This faith is not given to justify but only to do miracles, wonders, and signs. Therefore, St. Paul says :

" If I had all faith so that I could move mountains and have not charity, I am nothing " (1 Corinthians 13, 2).

According to Matthew, chapter seven, certain men shall say to Christ : " Behold we have done miracles and cast out devils in Thy name." Yet He shall say to them truly, I know you not. This faith is a gift of God that does not justify any more than the gift of knowledge or the gift of prophecies. This gift is in the church sometimes, and sometimes not. It is not there of necessity. But the faith that we speak of sticks fast to the blood of Christ and has no other virtue but to justify. It must justify, and wherever it is, it sticks fast to God's Word so firmly that it does not look for miracles. This faith is never out of the church for it is the life of the church. It is the faith that our Master Christ prayed for that it might never fail. Therefore, when St. Paul describes this faith, he calls it a faith that works by charity, not a faith that justifies by charity. As he says plainly, it is neither circumcision nor yet uncircumcision that is of any value in Christ Jesus, but faith (Galatians 5, 6). Here he plainly excludes from justification the highest work of the law, circumcision, and puts faith alone. Not the gift of faith that does miracles, but the gift of faith that works by charity.

St. Augustine supports my view in saying that there are two kinds of faith. One is justifying faith, of which it is said, " Thy faith hath saved thee." The other is called the gift of God whereby miracles are done. Of this it is said, " If you have faith as a grain of mustard seed." There you have a plain statement that faith alone justifies. Justification is only promised to that faith that is freely given of God. Nevertheless, this faith, in time and place convenient, is of such strength that it must perform acts of charity.

You have another argument in which you say that faith does not justify. True it is that we do not mean that faith justifies us for the sake of its own dignity or perfection. But

Scripture says that faith alone justifies because it is that through which alone I cling to Christ.. By faith alone I am partaker of the merits and mercy purchased by Christ's blood. It is faith alone that receives the promises made in Christ. Through our faith the merits, goodness, grace, and favour of Christ are imputed and reckoned to us. Our justice is not a formal justice which is deserved by us by the fulfilling of the law. If it were, our justification would not be of grace. It is a justice that is reckoned and imputed to us through faith in Christ Jesus. It is clearly, fully, and by mercy imputed to us.

Now, most honourable and gracious king, I have declared to your highness what faith it is that justifies us before God. I have brought for proof not only the blessed Word of God, which were sufficient for this purpose, but the exposition of the doctors that your grace might see that I am not moved to this opinion for insufficient reasons, and that my doctrine is not as new as men have called it. Moreover, I have declared to your grace how I would have good works done, and would not have a Christian's life to be an idle thing or a life of uncleanness, but would have them changed to all virtue and goodness and to live in good works after the commandment of God.

Your grace will perceive that my adversaries have not reported truly of me when they have said that I would forbid men to fast, pray, give alms, and be penitent for their sins. I have never taught or said such things and take God as witness with my works, my deeds, and all my writings. Therefore if it please your grace to hear me I will prove these charges to be untrue. This almighty God knows to be true. May He preserve your most royal majesty in honour and goodness. Amen.

2

THE CHURCH*

What The Church Is, Who Be Thereof, and Whereby Men May Know Her

IF a man will compare our Master Christ, who is the very head of holy church, with some prelates who call themselves His vicars, he shall find but small similarity between them. He that will consider Saints Peter and Paul and other apostles will realize that either they were not of the church, or our prelates are not, for they are similar in nothing. Yes, one may reckon that St. Peter and St. Paul were fools and madmen that lived such a contemptible life. What need is there to make many words or tell the names ? There is no doubt they will betray themselves. If the devil would come disguised, how could he be more contrary to Christ and His apostles than those men that call themselves the holy church? Therefore I will, by God's grace, describe what the holy church is and whereby men shall know her.

The word *ecclesia,* both in the New Testament and the Old, is often used for the whole congregation and the whole multitude of the people, both good and bad, as in Numbers 20, 4. " Why have you brought up the congregation of the Lord into this wilderness ? " and in 1 Kings 8, 14, " The king

* *See note on page 103*

37

turned his face and blessed the whole congregation of the
church of Israel, and all the church of Israel stood." Likewise, in the New Testament St. Paul writes to the Corinthians
(1 Corinthians 4, 17), " I have sent unto you Timothy, who
shall teach you my ways which are in Christ Jesus, as I do
teach everywhere in all congregations." In another place
St. Paul writes (1 Corinthians 11, 22) : " Do you despise the
congregation of God and shame them that have not ? " In
all these places and many more it is clear that the Greek
work *ecclesia* is used for the whole congregation both of good
and bad men. Therefore, this is not the church that we will
speak of, for in this church there are Jews and Saracens,
murderers and thieves, bawds and harlots, though we know
or recognize them not.

But there is another holy church of which St. Paul speaks.
" You men love your wives, as Christ has loved the church,
and has given himself for her, that he might sanctify her, and
cleanse her in the fountain of water through the word of life,
to make her to himself a glorious church without spot or
wrinkle or any such thing, but that she might be holy, and
without blame " (Ephesians 5, 25). Here you have the very
true church of Christ that is pure and clean without spot.

But whereby is she pure and clean ? Not by her own
merits nor by her own might, not by external array, not by
gold nor silver, nor yet by precious stones. Not by mitres
nor by the archbishop's cross-staff, nor by any other ecclesiastical symbols. Whereby, then ? By Christ only, who has
given Himself to make her clean. St. Paul says : " He gave
himself that he might sanctify her, that he might cleanse her,
and make her to himself a glorious church " (Ephesians 5,
25-27). In another place he says : " You are washed, you
are sanctified, you are justified in the name of Jesus Christ
and in the spirit of God " (1 Corinthians 6, 11). See, my
lords, how the church is washed by Christ and by His Holy

Spirit, and not by your spiritual holy water, for these things cannot help the holy church. She is holy in spirit and not in outward hypocrisy; she is cleansed by Christ's blessed blood, and not by outward disguises.

This St. Augustine well proves, saying : " Of Christ is the church made fair. At first she was filthy in sins, afterward by pardon and grace she was made fair." Here St. Augustine says that Christ has made His church fair and that by His grace and His pardon, not by your pardons nor by your grace. This church stands in Christ's election, and not by yours. If Christ has not washed you and chosen you, then you are not of this church, though you ride with a thousand spiritual horses and have all the spiritual tokens on earth. If the Son of God has delivered you, then you are truly delivered. You cannot by all your power and holiness make good ale or wine out of green fruit. Will you then, with your spiritual signs and tokens, make the church of God follow you, or by these signs and tokens, determine where the church shall be ? Nay, nay, my lords, it will not be. But they that believe that Christ has washed them from their sins, and stick fast to His merits and to the promise made to them in Him, they are the church of God. They are so pure and clean that it shall not be lawful, not even for Peter, to say that they are unclean. Whether they be Jew or Greek, king or subject, carter or cardinal, butcher or bishop, water boy or street sweeper, free or bound, friar or fiddler, monk or miller; if they believe in Christ's Word and stick fast to His blessed promises, and trust only in the merits of His blessed blood, they are the Holy church of God, yea and the very true church before God.

You, with all your spiritual tokens and with all your external cleanness, remain in the filthiness of your sin. From that sin all your blessings, all your pardons, all your spirituality, and all your holiness cannot cleanse you or bring you into this church. Boast, brag, blast, bless, curse till your holy eyes start out of your head. It will not help you for Christ chooses His church at His judgment and not at yours. The Holy Ghost is free, and enlightens where He will. He will neither be bound to pope nor cardinal, archbishop nor bishop, abbot nor prior, deacon nor archdeacon, parson nor vicar, nun nor friar.

Briefly, come all the whole rabble of you that call yourselves the holy church and exclude all others, yea and take sun, moon and stars to help you with all the friends you have in heaven and earth, and you shall not be members of the holy church unless you have the Spirit of Christ and are washed in His holy blood. For the holy church of Christ is nothing else but that congregation which is sanctified in spirit, redeemed with Christ's blood, and sticks fast and sure only to the promises that are made therein.

The church is spiritual, and not an external thing. It is invisible from carnal eyes. I do not say that they are invisible who are of the church, but that the holy church in herself is invisible. It is invisible as faith is invisible, and her pureness and cleanness is before Christ only and not before the world, for the world has no understanding or knowledge of her. All her honour and cleanness is sure and fast before Christ. If any of her goodness appears to the world, she makes no virtue of it; she does not think herself anything the better because the world thinks well of her, for all her trust is in Christ only. She suffers the world to rage and to blaspheme both against her and against Christ, her Maker. She stands fast and believes steadfastly that this hostility will have a shameful end and the reward of everlasting damnation. Briefly, her meditations and her thoughts are heavenly, and all that she does is spiritual. She cannot err because she cleaves fast to the Word of God which is the truth.

For this cause St. Paul calls her the pillar and ground of

truth because she sticks so fast to the living God and to His blessed Word. This is the very true church that is scattered through all the world. It is neither bound to a person by reason of dignity, nor yet to any place by reason of a feigned holiness. She is a free thing through all the world. St. Augustine witnesses to this in these words : " We are the holy church, but not only we who are here and who do hear my words now, but all who are faithful Christians in this congregation, that is to say, in this city, in this region, beyond the sea, and in all the world. From the rising of the sun to its setting God's name is praised and the holy church is our mother."

From these words it is plain that the holy church is the congregation of faithful men wherever they are in the world. Neither the pope nor yet his cardinals are more this church or of this church than the poorest man on earth. This church stands solely in the spiritual faith of Christ Jesus, and not in dignities or honours of the world, as Lyra declares in these words : " The church does not stand in men by reason of spiritual power or secular dignities. Many princes and popes, and many inferior persons have swerved from the faith. The church stands in those persons who have the true knowledge and make a true confession of faith and of truth."

Oh, my lords, what will you say to Lyra ? I marvel that you do not burn him. It is high time to condemn him for heresy for he speaks against your law. Your commentaries declare that God does not suffer the church of Rome to err. And Lyra says plainly that many popes have erred, and that the church does not stand on its dignity, but in the confession of Christ and His blessed truth.

Here it will be objected that, like our logicians, I imagine a church that does not exist. Where shall a man find a church that is so pure and so clean that it has neither spot nor wrinkle in her, and is without sin, since all men must of

truth say "forgive us our trespasses" ? If any man, be he
ever so righteous, says that he has no sin, he is a liar, and
there is no truth in him. To this I answer that this holy
church has sin in her, and yet she is pure and clean. Mark
St. Paul's words : "Christ has given himself for her that he
might make her glorious" (Ephesians 5, 25-27).

So that the cleanness of this holy church is the mercy of
God toward her through Christ, for whose sake He lays
nothing to her charge. Between them all is common, as
between man and wife. So if the church looks on her own
merits and her own works, she is full of sin and must say
"forgive me my sins". This she would not need to say if she
had no sins.

If she refers herself to the merits of her blessed husband,
Christ Jesus, and to the cleanness that she has in His blood,
then she is without spot. Because she sticks fast to her
husband Christ, by faith, abides in the confession of her sins
and requires mercy for them, nothing is laid to her charge;
everything is forgiven her.

The church abides in prayer that she might be cleansed by
acknowledging her sins. Here you see clearly that the church
of God is cleansed and purified by Christ for the satisfaction
of her sins and that not by her own pureness. Such a church
there must be, though the carnal eye cannot see her, nor
can fleshly reason judge her. Therefore, we believe as an
article of faith that the holy church is a communion or
fellowship of holy men. We know it is not by seeing or
feeling as we know a fellowship of drapers or mercers, for
then it would not be an article of faith.

It is plain that all your external signs, with all your holy
ornaments, such as your holy mitres, your holy cross-staves,
your holy pillars, your holy red gloves, your holy adornments,
your holy rings, your holy anointed fingers, your holy vest-
ments, your holy chalices, and your holy golden shoes; yea,

and if you also take the holy shoes of St. Thomas of Canterbury with all the holy boots of holy monks, all these together cannot make one crumb of holiness in you, nor help you one iota forward toward being in this church. For if these things could help, then it would be simple to make an ass to be of the church of God.

Our holy mother the church has another holiness that comes from God the Father through the sweet blood of His blessed Son Jesus Christ, in whom she has all her confidence and trust. To Him alone she holds fast in steadfast faith. By His purity she is pure, though confessing her own uncleanness. She believes that she has an advocate for her sin before the Father in heaven, who is Christ Jesus and that He is the satisfaction for her sins. Of His mercy, and not because of her merits, He has chosen her to be His. Because she is His, she must be clean so long as she abides in Him.

This is well declared in St. John where our Master is compared to the vine and all the members of holy church to the branches. As the branches can bring forth no fruit of themselves, so can the holy church of herself bring forth no goodness except she remain in Christ by perfect faith (John 15, 5).

This is well proved by your own law, whose words are these : " The church is holy because she believes righteously in God." Do you not see what makes the church holy ? It is because she believes righteously in God; that is, she believes in nothing but in Him and she neither believes nor hears any word but His, as our Master Christ bears witness : " My sheep hear my voice, and another man's voice they do not know " (John 10, 3-5). In another place He says : " He that is of God hears the words of God " (John 8, 47). Why does the church of God have so sure a discernment that she knows the voice of Christ from other voices and cannot err in her judgment ? It is because Christ has chosen her, and because she has been taught by God, as our Master Christ says. It is, as St. John says, because she has the inward ointment of God and has been taught all truth so that she cannot err. But why can she not err since she may do what she will ? Is it because everything that she does is well done, because she may make new rules and new laws at her pleasure ? Is it because she may invent a new service of God, that is not in Scripture, at her will ? Nay, my lords, for she is but a woman and must be ruled by her husband. Yes, she is but a sheep and must hear the voice of her shepherd, and as long as she does she cannot err because the voice of her shepherd cannot be false.

This may be proved by your own law whose words are these : " The whole church cannot err. The congregation of believing men cannot err." These words make plain which church it is that cannot err, that is, the congregation of believing men who are gathered in Christ's name, which have Christ's spirit, which have the holy ointment of God, which abide fast by Christ's word, and hear no other man's voice than His. Now, my lords, gather together all the laws that you can make and all the holiness that you can devise, and cry, " The Church, the Church; the Councils, the Councils that were lawfully gathered in the power of the Holy Ghost." All this you may say and yet lie if you have not the Holy Ghost within you. If you hear any other voice than Christ's, then you are not of the church, but of the devil, and are thieves and murderers as Christ says. You come unto the fold without Him. You bring not His voice, but you come with your own voice, with your own statutes, and with your own word.

These are the voices of murderers and thieves, and not of Christ. Therefore, you cannot fail to err because you are not taught by God; you do not have the holy ointment, you do not have the Word of God, you do not hear the voice of the true Shepherd. You must needs err, therefore, in all your counsels. This is another kind of rule than that which my Lord of Rochester establishes to test your counsels by. He says that where the pope and council do not agree he will suspect that the council is not right.

Who did ever hear such a rule of a Christian man, yes, and he a bishop and a doctor of divinity ? Where has he learned a divinity that regards a council as true because the pope and so many men agree ? He thinks that the Council of Constantinople, which had three hundred and thirty bishops, erred because the pope did not agree with it. Let him read his own laws and he shall find that the pope has erred. Why, then, should the validity of a council depend on his judgment ? How will he save the Councils of Constance and Basel by this rule, both of which condemned popes as heretics ? Since these Councils mention that councils have erred, he will probably say that they were not full councils.

Concerning the truth in a council that has a thousand bishops and in another which has five thousand, it may well be asked whether the multitude of men determines the truth. Then the Turk would have the truth and we the falsehood. Then the prophets of Baal had the truth and not Elijah, for they were four hundred and fifty and he was but one man.

Christ's flock always has the smallest number in this world, but yet it is the best. Yet not the smallest number makes Christ's flock, for His church stands neither by the greater number nor yet by the smallest, nor by the judgment or numbering of men, but by the calling and election of God. Therefore let my lord bring forth whatever council he will, if it has not the Word of God I will not only say that it may err, but also that it does surely err. In matters of faith the affirmation of a private person is to be preferred before that

of a pope if he has better reasons, and if he has the Old
and New Testaments on his side.

Nor can it help to say that a council cannot err because
Christ did pray for His church that her faith should not
fail.   I answer to this that though the general council
represents the whole universal church, yet it is not the very
universal church, but only its representative.   The universal
church stands in the election of all believing men, for all believing men of the world make the universal church whose
head and spouse is Christ Jesus.   The pope is but the vicar
of Christ and not the very head of the church.

It is clear that a council may err, and that a person having
Scripture on his side is to be heard before the pope or a
council having no Scripture on their side.   You have, therefore, the very true church which cannot err and which cannot
be verified by your councils for they are neither free from
error nor are they the holy church.   They represent the
church as a legate represents a king's person.   From that it
does not follow that the legate is the king, that he has as
much power as the king, or that he is above his king or may
rule him.   Augustine says that those councils which are
gathered in every province must without doubt give place
to full councils of all Christendom, and also that those full
councils must often be amended by the full councils that
come later if anything is revealed by later experience or
knowledge that was previously hidden.   This may be done
without a shadow of superstitious pride, without any boasted
arrogance, without any contention of malicious envy, but with
holy meekness, with holy peace, and with Christian charity.

It is clear that full councils may be amended and reformed.
This would not be necessary if they could not err, yea and if
indeed they did not err.   Moreover, you must grant that
there is a rule whereby your councils must be examined and
whereby sentence must be given as to which are true and

which are false. If your councils are not ordered by this rule, they must err and be false and of the devil. Therefore, gather all your councils together, and yet of these you cannot make a church.

But perhaps there may be, in your councils, many good and perfect men of the holy church. Yet they and you together do not make the universal holy church that cannot err. Neither have you any authority over the church beyond the Word of God. As soon as you forsake Christ and His holy Word, so soon are you the congregation of the devil and are thieves and murderers. And yet for all this there must needs be an holy church of Christ on earth that is neither bound to Jerusalem, nor to Constantinople, nor yet to Rome.

It will be objected that our Master Christ commands that, if my brother offend me, I should complain to the church. But how can a man complain to a church which is spiritual, when no man knows but God only, and is scattered throughout the world ? I answer that our Master Christ does plainly speak of a man who has suffered an injustice who, therefore, must be a particular and certain man. Therefore, God bids him complain not to the universal church, but to a particular church.

Now this particular church, if it is of God, and is a true member of the universal church, will judge righteously in accordance with Christ's Word the cause brought before her. Nevertheless, it often comes to pass that this particular church does fully and wholly err, and judges unrighteously and excommunicates him who is blessed of God. Your own laws indicate this in the words " oft times he that is cast out is within, and he that is within is kept without ". Here you see plainly how a particular church may err. Therefore, the only church that cannot err is the universal church which is called the communion and fellowship of saints.

Now I have declared unto you what the holy church is,

that is, the congregation of believing men throughout all the world, and wherein she is holy, that is, by Christ's holiness and by Christ's blood, and also why she cannot err, because she keeps herself fast to the Word of God which is a perfect and a true rule.

Now we must declare by what signs and tokens we may know that in this place or in that place there are certain members of this holy church. Though in herself the church is spiritual and cannot be perfectly known by our external senses, yet we may have certain tokens of her spiritual presence whereby we may reckon that in this place and in that place there are certain of her members. As by a natural example, though the soul of man in herself is spiritual and invisible, yet may we have sure tokens of her presence such as hearing, moving, speaking, and smelling. So likewise, where the word of God is truly and perfectly preached without the damnable dreams of men, and where it is well received of its hearers, and also where we see good works that do openly agree with the doctrine of the gospel, these are good and sure tokens whereby we may judge that there are some men of the holy church.

As to the first, where the gospel is truly preached it must needs light in some men's hearts, as the prophet witnesses (Isaiah 55, 11) : " My word shall not return again to me frustrate, but it shall do everything that I will, and it shall prosper in those things unto which I did send it."

St. Paul also says (Romans 10, 17) : " Faith cometh by hearing, and hearing cometh by the word of God." Therefore it is clear in holy Scriptures that when Peter spoke the words of God, the Holy Ghost descended on them all. Therefore, it is plain that God's Word can never be preached in vain. Some men must needs receive it and thereby come into the holy church, though men do not know them either by their names nor yet by their faces, for the Word is received into their hearts.

The second token is that the receivers of this Word do good works thereafter. St. Paul declares of his hearers (1 Thess. 2, 13) : " When you received of us the word wherewith God was preached, you received it not as the word of men, but even (as indeed it was) the word of God, which worketh in you that believe." So that if men do good works according to the Word of God, it is a good token that in that place are men of the church, though (hypocrisy is so subtle and so secret) we may be often deceived by these outward works.

There is no other way for them that will know which is the very true church of Christ, except through the Scriptures. From the beginning the church of Christ was made known through the conversation of Christian men, either of all or of many who were holy. Wicked men did not have this holiness. But now Christian men are as evil or worse than heretics and Gentiles, yes, and greater continence is found among them than among Christian men.

Therefore, he that will know which is the very church of Christ, how shall he know it, but by Scripture only ? Therefore, our Lord, knowing that so great a confusion of things should come in the latter days, commanded that Christian men which are in Christendom and are willing to preserve the steadfastness of true faith should flee unto no other thing but unto the Scriptures. If they have respect unto other things, they shall be deceived and shall perish, not understanding which is the true church.

These words need no exposition. They are plain enough. They exclude all manner of learning except holy Scripture, and therefore wheresoever the Word of God is preached it is a good token that there are some men of Christ's church. As to the fruits and works of this church, her manner of living and all her good works, they are taken out of the

holy Word of God.   The church does not dream any other
new holiness or newly invented works that are not in Scripture, but she is content with Christ's teaching and believes
that Christ has sufficiently taught her every kind of good
work that is to the honour of our heavenly Father.   Therefore,
she invents no other way to heaven but follows Christ alone
in suffering oppressions, persecutions, blasphemies and all
other things which may be laid to her charge.   St. Augustine
says : " The church learned from our Master Christ.   Our
holy mother, the church, scattered far and long throughout
the world, taught through her true head Christ Jesus, has
learned not to fear scorn of the cross nor yet death.   More
and more she is strengthened, not in resisting, but in
suffering."

Now, my lords, compare yourselves to this rule of St.
Augustine and let us see how you can bring yourselves into
the church or prove yourselves to be holy.   The church
suffers persecution (for as St. Paul says, " All that will live
devoutly in Christ must suffer persecution " 2 Tim. 3, 12),
and you withstand all things and suffer nothing.   You oppress
every man, and you will be opposed by no man.   You
persecute every man, and no man may speak a word against
you, though it be ever so true.   You cast every man in
prison, and no man may touch you but he shall be cursed.
You compel every man to say as you say, and you will not
once say as Christ says.   And as for your holiness, all the
world knows what it is, for it consists in clothing and in
ornamentation, in watching and sleeping, in eating and drinking this meat or that meat, this drink or that drink, in
pattering and mumbling these psalms or those without
devotion.

Briefly all your holiness is in books, bells, candles, chalices,
oil cream, water, horses, hounds, palaces, and all that is
mighty and glorious in the world.   On these you build, in

these you glory, of these you brag and boast. Is this the nature of the church ? Is this holiness ? Of whom have you learned this conduct ? You cannot deny that these things are true, and, if you would deny it, all the world is witness against you, yes, and also your own actions and deeds.

But let us see what St. Bernard says about you. " They call themselves the ministers of Christ, but they serve Anti-christ. They go gorgeously arrayed in our Lord's goods, unto whom they give no honour. Of the Lord's goods comes the harlots' finery, the actors' costumes, and the royal apparel that you see daily. From this source comes the gold in their bridles, in their saddles, and in their spurs, so that their spurs are brighter than their altars. From this wealth come their plenteous wine presses, their full cellars, bulging with many things. From this come their barrels of sweet wines, and of this supply of the Lord are their bags filled. For such things as these are they rulers of the church, deacons, archdeacons, bishops and archbishops."

My lords, I had thought to have added cardinals and legates, abbots and priors, to have made the company more holy, but I dared not. Now think you. Of whom does St. Bernard speak when he says bishops and archbishops ? What holiness does he reprove when he speaks of gorgeous array, of harlots' finery, of actors' costumes, of golden spurs, saddles and bridles ? If there were a hundred who did fit the description more than you, you would still be obliged to admit that he speaks of you. He far surpasses me in condemning your holy ornaments, for he calls you the servants of Anti-christ and speaks of your actors' costumes and says that you are neither the church nor of the church, but the servants of Anti-christ. What think you of St. Bernard ? It is time to condemn him because he speaks against the holy church and all her ornaments. This dare I well say that if the best

Christian men within the realm should preach these words of Saint Bernard, you would not hesitate to condemn him for an heretic. You are accustomed to call him sweet Bernard, but I think he is sour enough in this matter. Therefore dispute the matter with him that you may come into the church rather than discuss it with me.

NOTE : Barnes is less precise than Luther in identifying the external and visible marks of the church. Barnes says in this essay that the church is present where " the Word of God is truly and perfectly preached . . . where it is well of the hearers received . . . and where we see good works that do openly agree with the doctrine of the Gospel." Luther did not accept good works as a mark of the church because, as he said, " External works can deceive, since after all they are found even among the heathen." For Luther the church was identified by the Word and the Sacraments alone. He said, " The external marks whereby one may perceive where this church is on earth, are Baptism, the Sacrament of the Altar, and the Gospel . . . ". Luther considered good works the fruit of the preaching of the true Gospel. He cautioned that " The church does not stand on the holiness of any one person ".

Barnes came nearer to Luther's definition when, some three years later, he defended his view of the doctrine of the church against the attack of Sir Thomas More.* He then stated that the marks of the church were present when " The Word of God is purely and sincerely preached and the Sacraments orderly ministered after the blessed ordinance of Christ ". To this, however, he added the words : " Where men patiently suffer for the truth and the hearers apply their living to Christ's doctrine and with meekness receive the holy Sacraments : These are good and perfect tokens to judge that in that place there are members of the church ". Barnes had come nearer to Luther in his second essay on the church, but he still did not make Luther's clear distinction between the marks of the church and the fruits of the use of the Word and the Sacraments.

* See note on page 103

3

THE OFFICE OF THE KEYS[*]

What The Keys Of The Church Be and
To Whom They Were Given

THE scholastic theologian Duns Scotus says that the keys of heaven are nothing else than an authority given to priests whereby they say that heaven shall be opened to this man and shut unto another so that heaven is opened and shut at the sentence of a priest. Who could have invented such a doctrine but the devil himself ? Who can speak greater heresy than this ? Who can speak more openly against Christ and His holy Scriptures ? If the authority of the priest himself is the key to heaven and can open and shut heaven, then no one can be saved without the authority of the priest. Then no priest can be damned, for he has the keys of heaven. I do not think priests would be so mad as to use their own authority to shut themselves in with the devil.

What need have we of Christ and His holy Word if the authority of the priest is the key of heaven ? I would ask you all where you can bring me one proof text from Scripture where the sentence of a priest has loosed a sinner or bound a righteous man. If he cannot do this, then there is an

* See note on page 105

authority above the sentence of a priest. It is further against
reason that his authority should be the keys of heaven, and
it is also contrary to his own doctrine. Both Duns and Lyra
plainly declare that your key of authority may err. Now, if
it may err, it is not the right key to the lock of heaven
because the right key can never err in its own lock. Therefore, the most you can make it is a picklock which belongs
to thieves and robbers only.

Moreover, if this were the key, then we would never be
certain whether heaven were opened or not. First, we have
no word or promise of God concerning this key. We cannot
know when it opens heaven and when it does not, for
according to the admission of your own doctors it may err.
If it shall chance to err, then the gates to heaven are not
opened. Thus we shall always be in doubt as to whether
we are loosed from our sins or not.

Therefore, we must seek out another key that is the very
true key to the lock, which cannot err, and of which we shall
be in all certainty and without any doubt. Before we declare
what this key is, we will first show the nature and the property
of this key.

This is nothing else than the holy Word of God through
which we receive faith into our hearts. St. Paul says : " Faith
is by hearing, and hearing is by the word of God " (Romans
10, 17). The Psalmist says : " The word is a lantern unto
my feet and it is a light unto my path " (Psalm 119, 105).
By this Word do we receive life as the prophet says : " Thy
speech shall quicken me " (Psalm 119, 25). The secrets of
our hearts are also opened by this Word.

St. Paul says that " if one comes who does not believe, he
is reproved by the word of all men, and the secrets of his
heart are opened " (1 Corinthians 14, 24-25). By this Word
grace and everlasting life is also declared unto us, as St. Paul
says : " Christ has put away death, and has brought life and

immortality to light through the gospel " (2 Timothy 1, 10).

It is through Christ that our conscience is loosed and made free from sin. Therefore the psalmist says, " There is much peace unto them that love the law of God and nothing shall offend them " (Psalm 119, 165). Much peace is nothing else than the remission of sins, yes, and that without any doubt because he that is loosed by the Word of God and has the clear Word of God saying that his sins are forgiven him can not be deceived. Nothing can make him doubt. Though heaven and hell, life and death do threaten him, he is not offended; he is not deceived; but holds fast and knows certainly that all these things must perish, but the Word of God abides forever. Therefore, this is the key that judges the thoughts and intent of the heart, as St. Paul says (Hebrews 4, 12). By this we also have the knowledge of our sin as St. Paul declares to the Romans (Romans 3, 20) and by this is also declared unto us grace and also remission of sins if we believe it.

This must be the very true key, as you may evidently see throughout all Scripture, and not your boasted and bragged power. There is not, and cannot be, anything in man that can loose his soul from his sin. Man is only a minister and dispenser of the heavenly Word of God. For the Word's sake our sins are remitted when we believe it, and retained when we despise it. Therefore, the blessed Word of God is the very key, and in it is all the might and power to loose our sins. Man is but a minister and servant to this Word.

This is evident from our Master Christ's words where He says, " Go your ways into all the world and preach the gospel unto all creatures, and he that doth believe and is baptized shall be saved, but he that doth not believe shall be damned " (Mark 16, 15-16). Apostles are but ministers and servants and have no power, save that of ministration. The key which they have, whereby they must loose and bind, is the very

Word of God. And, therefore our Master Christ says that he
that believeth shall be saved, and he that doth not believe
shall be damned. By this Word the holy apostles declared
grace through Christ and taught men to set all their hope of
salvation in Christ alone. By this Word they taught men to
acknowledge their sin and to seek for grace, and fully and
wholly to hope for forgiveness of their sins in Christ alone.
Where this key is received by faith there all things are loosed,
all sins forgiven, and consciences are made free.

In this manner the holy apostles did bind and loose when
they preached the holy Word of God to the people. Peter
preached this holy Word, and at his preaching the hearers
were pricked in their hearts and asked Peter what they might
do. He answered, " Repent and be baptized every one of
you in the name of Jesus for the remission of your sins and
you shall receive the gift of the Holy Ghost." Therefore as
many as received His Word were baptized.

This is the manner of loosing from sins as the holy apostles
practised it. When the people believed the Word that they
preached, then the apostles declared that their sins were
remitted for Christ's sake and not through any power that
they had, because they were only ministers. The power was
in the Word of God through which they were delivered from
their sins. This is evident from our Master Christ's word in
which He says to them, " Go and preach, the kingdom of
heaven is at hand " (Matthew 10, 7). His words follow :
" In what house you enter, say first, peace be with you, and
if the house is worthy your peace shall come on it " (Matthew
10, 12-13). That is to say, if they receive your word and
believe it, then shall your peace, that is the peace of the
Gospel which you bring with you, give them quietness of
conscience and loose them from all sin. But if the house
is not worthy, your peace shall return to you again, and
whosoever shall not receive you, nor will hear your preaching,

when you depart out of that house, shake the dust from your feet. I say it shall be easier for Sodom and Gomorrah in the day of judgment than for that house.

It cannot be doubted that many men were loosed from their sin by hearing the apostles preaching the Word of God and yet never spoke with the apostles. Therefore, receiving of the Word, not the apostles, loosed them from their sins.

Now you see clearly how the holy apostles did bind and loose, and with what key they did it. It was by the preaching of the holy Word of God. And so that this thing might be done without any error, and so that no man should doubt of it He gave them the Holy Ghost, saying, " Whose sins you do forgive shall be forgiven, and whose sins ye retain shall be retained " (John 20, 23-24). To these words Luke adds : " Then opened he their wit that they might understand the Scriptures " (Luke 24, 45).

It is writen in Luke that " Christ must suffer death and rise again the third day, and that repentance and remission of sins should be preached in his name among all nations " (Luke 24, 46-47). Now what St. John says in the words " Whose sins you do loose shall be loosed " Luke says in the words " remission of sins must be preached in his name ". To say that " whose sins you do loose shall be loosed " is the same as to say that you must " preach remission of sins in my name ". As many as receive this Word shall be loosed by this Word, and as many as do not receive it shall be bound by the same Word.

Thus the apostles did bind and loose by preaching the Word of God. They did bind with the Word when it was not believed. They did loose with the Word when it was believed. Thus, by one Word, they preached both salvation and damnation, but to different men. This virtue of the Word St. Paul declared in these words : " We are unto God the sweet savour among them which perish. To the one part we are the savour of death unto death, unto the other part we are the savour unto life." What is this savour ? It is nothing else but the Gospel, which to one is the loosing and remission of sins, and to another the occasion of binding and retaining in sin. Paul declares this in another place, saying : " The preaching of the cross is to them that perish foolishness. But unto us which are saved it is the power of God " (1 Corinthians 1, 18). What is this power of God ? Nothing else but remission and loosing from our sins. What is foolishness ? Nothing else but that they despise the Gospel and reckon it to be of no value and of no power. Therefore, they remain bound in this sin.

Thus it is that one word of God works diverse operations in diverse men. In one it works life, that is, forgiveness of sins. In the other it works death and is taken for foolishness, that is, it declares them bound and retained in their damnable sins. The diversity is in the receivers of the Word. This may be illustrated from nature. The dew of heaven comes down impartially on all the ground. But in one it brings forth good corn and sweet fruits. In the other it brings forth nettles and brambles that are worth nothing but only for the fire.

In the same way the preaching of the holy Word of God, when it is believed, quiets and looses our consciences from all sin through Christ. When it is not believed, it binds us and retains us in sin. Thus the holy Word is the very true key of heaven, for by it heaven is opened and shut.

We have seen that by believing the Word of God our sins are loosed and that by unbelief we are bound in our sins. Now we must see to whom the keys are given. They were not only given to Peter, for then Paul and the two Sons of Thunder, James and John, would not have had them. Nor may they be given to one more than to another, for Christ was impartial and they were all His apostles and their confession was all one. Therefore, no doubt these keys were given to all Christ's apostles and to the whole church.

Peter received the keys in the name of the church. Therefore they belong to all Christian men. The words, " Thou art Peter " were spoken unto Peter, unto all apostles, and unto all manner of faithful men, for they are all *Peter,* and in them is built the church of Christ, and against none of them can the gates of hell prevail.

Here it will be clearly seen that all Christians are Peter. They have all received the keys of heaven, and hell cannot prevail against them. St. Augustine testifies to this in the words : " Therefore the church which is founded and grounded in Christ has received from Him the keys of heaven, that is to say, the power to bind and loose."

Thus it is plain that those keys are given to the whole church of Christ. They are the common treasure of the church and belong no more to one man than to another. Because all men cannot use these keys all together, for that would cause confusion, therefore the church, that is the congregation of faithful men, commits the ministration of those keys, that is the preaching of God's Word, to certain men whom they think most able and learned in the Word of God. The men thus chosen are but ministers of the common treasure and are not lords over it. The church may depose them, that is she may take away the common ministration that she committed unto them if they do not use it well. Then they are as other Christian men, having no common office or administration in the church.

Therefore, they may neither preach nor yet minister the sacraments publicly. They may only do as other Christian men may do privately in their own houses or in other places where men are gathered which will hear of Christ. There, I say, both they and other Christian men may speak and teach Christ's Word and declare it in accordance with the gift given them of God. They that do believe this Word thus preached by Christian men are, by the power of the keys, loosed from their sin. They are bound if they do not believe. For all the church and every part of the church has power to execute these keys, saving that good order be not broken. This St. Paul declares, saying that all may interpret Scripture, but that all things must be done " decently and in order " (1 Corinthians 14, 40).

Now, to keep good order, and so that nothing should be done in confusion, the church assigns certain men as the public ministers of this treasure. But they are only ministers and not lords. It is a common treasury and not a private treasure. St. Paul says, " Let a man so reckon us as the ministers of Christ and the stewards of the ministry of God " (1 Corinthians 4, 1). He adds, " What is St. Paul, what is Apollos, but ministers by whom you have believed " (1 Corinthians 3, 5).

St. Peter also commands that bishops and priests should not exercise any dominion over the congregations, but give example to the flock (1 Peter 5, 3). Are these not plain Scriptures showing that you are no lords, but ministers of Christ's treasure ? Nevertheless you leave the ministration and usurp authority.

St. Peter commands that priests should only be ministers and bearers of these keys. St. Chrysostom proves this in the words : " The key bearers are priests to whom is committed the teaching of the Word and the interpretation of Scripture." St. Ambrose testifies to this when he says : " Sins are forgiven by the Word of God whose interpreter is the deacon."

Where now is your lordly power which you call the keys of heaven ? Is not the Scripture, the practice of the Apostles, and the expositions of the holy doctors against you ? Will you usurp a thing that is contrary to all these ? Where in all Scripture do you find Peter or Paul absolving sins after the manner of your keys ? Yet, no doubt, they had the keys and did use them. Therefore, it is a great marvel to me to know from whom you have learned your usage. Where have you gotten such keys ? It does not matter that you may support your practice by the fathers, the councils, and the church. I have the holy Word of God and our Master Christ and they are older than the fathers. I have also the practice of the holy apostles and they understand this matter better than all your councils.

I put before you the example of a prisoner bound fast in chains, over whom the king has given you the custody and keeping. Now the king's grace says to you, " Loose that fellow and let him go free out of prison under this condition that he shall promise to serve no other prince." Will you loose him or not ? Can you, or dare you, keep him longer if you would ? Can you make any other condition with him than to serve the king alone ? If you keep him in prison longer, do you not risk the king's displeasure ? And, if the prisoner makes any other condition for his release with you, is he bound to it ? What power have you, by your own authority, to release him ? Yes, what are you but the king's minister, a servant to the poor fellow in your custody ? The ministration and service is yours, but the authority is the king's.

Thus the Word of God which carries pardon for all sinners is committed to you to preach and declare. If your hearers receive it in faith, they are free and loosed from their sins. If they do not receive it, they are bound, and that not by your authority, for you are ministers and servants and can go no further than your commission but by God's authority alone.

4

FREE WILL AND ELECTION*

Free Will of Man, After The Fall of Adam, of His Natural Strength, Can Do Nothing but Sin Before God.

IN this article we will not discuss what man may do through the ordinary abilities given him by God. We shall not be concerned about his powers over commonplace and temporal things such as eating and drinking, sleeping and speaking, buying and selling, and in all such natural abilities as are given impartially by God to all men. We shall rather inquire what strength man has, of his natural power without the Spirit of God, to do those things that are acceptable to God toward the fulfilment of His will. We shall be concerned about the ability of man to believe in God, to love God according to His commandments, to love justice for itself, to take God for his Father, to reckon God to be merciful to him, to fear God lovingly, and with other things that men call good works.

That man can do nothing in these causes by his free will our Master Christ proves in these words : " He that abideth in me, and I in him, bringeth forth much fruit, for without me ye can do nothing : if a man abide not in me, he is cast out as a branch and shall burn " (John 15, 5-6).

See note on page 105

Here it is clear that free will without grace can do nothing that is fruitful, or meritorious before God. He that has not Christ in him is cast out. This is the first fruit of free will. The second fruit is that he withers and this withering contributes nothing to his goodness. Finally he is gathered and cast into the fire. This is the third fruit. In the fire he can do nothing but burn. He cannot lie in the fire and ignore it. He must burn, and he cannot come out of the fire by his own strength. Let him desire escape as much as he will, his desire will not help him or further his escape. Therefore, left to his own fate, all the might of free will leaves no issue but first to be cast out, second to wither and decay, and third to be cast onto the fire. Matters go from bad to worse. Finally he burns, and this is worst of all, for in the fire he is past help. The strength that he has in his free will is only to bring himself to utter destruction.

Let us see how St. Augustine understands the text of St. John that we have referred to. Lest anyone should suppose that the branch could bring forth at least a little fruit, we should observe that Christ does not say that without Me you can do a little, but He says without Me ye can do nothing. Therefore, whether it be little or much, it cannot be done without Him without Whom nothing is done. The branch must do one of two things. Either is must abide in the vine or else burn in the fire. If it is not in the vine, it is in the fire. Without grace, free will can do neither little nor much. If it is not in Christ, it must burn in the fire.

St. Paul says that we are not sufficient to think anything of ourselves, but our sufficiency is of God (2 Corinthians 3, 5). What can be a smaller thing than to think ? And yet this small thing we cannot do. It is clear that St. Paul does not refer to the thinking that is our natural ability. Here he speaks of such thinking as is acceptable and praiseworthy before God. He is speaking of that thinking that is a unique and special gift of God, and not of the common gift of nature.

Christ asks : " Shall men gather grapes of thorns or figs of bramble bushes ?   An evil tree can bring forth no good fruit " (Matthew 7, 5).   What does our Master mean when He says that grapes are not gathered from thorns ? Nothing else than that the fruit must be like the tree.   Therefore He says that an evil tree cannot bring forth good fruit.   Now you cannot deny that free will without grace is an evil tree. Therefore its fruit must be evil.   It may bring forth fruit, but the fruit will not be good.   Is not all the power of free will expressed in these words ?

Our Master said to the Pharisees : " How can you that are evil speak good things ? " (Matthew 12, 34).   You reckon it but a small thing to speak good, yet, small as it is free will is not capable of it.   How should his speech be good who himself is evil ?   How should he do good that does not know what good is ?

You also have an accepted principle that nothing is loved and desired but that which is known.   Now how should free will flee from sin and desire goodness when it does not know what is sin and what is not ?   St. Paul says : " By the law is the knowledge of sin " (Romans 3, 20).   Free will is so blind that it does not recognize sin as sin or virtue as virtue, but regards that which is evil as good and that which is good as evil because it is lost and has no true judgment.   St. Augustine asks what good he who is lost can do except that he be delivered from his misery.   Can he do good by his free will ?   God forbid, for man using his free will evilly both loses himself and his free will.   When a man, alive, kills himself, he cannot make himself alive again.   So likewise, when man sins by his free will and sin has the victory, then free will is completely lost.

St. Augustine declares what free will deserves without grace when he says : " O cursed free will without God. Behold, man was made good, and by his free will he made himself evil. How shall an evil man who forsakes God by his free will now make himself good when he that was good could not keep himself good ? " Experience teaches that we have been made miserable by the exercise of free will and yet we boast our free will. Shall we call it blessed ? St. Paul says : " The wisdom of the flesh is an enemy of God, it is not subject to the law, nor can be, for they that serve the flesh cannot please God. And he that hath not the Spirit of Christ, the same man is none of his : for the same spirit beareth witness to our spirit that we are the children of God " (Romans 8, 7-16). Here you see plainly that the wisdom of the flesh is enmity against God. This St. Paul affirms when he says : " He that hath not the spirit of Christ, the same is not Christ's " (Romans 8, 9). In these words it is clear that reason, wisdom, heart, or whatever is in man (without the Spirit of God) is but flesh and cannot be obedient. He does not say that he will not, but that he cannot. He has no might, he has no power, even though he intend his best, do all that lies in him with all his might and all his power, it still cannot please God for it is only of the flesh.

Here the scholastic theologians will make a distinction and say that the word flesh here refers to fleshly desires and voluptuousness only, not to the desires of the soul nor the election of the will. I would know what part of man it is that is covetous or voluptuous. It is not the bones, nor the sinews, nor the flesh attached to them, but the highest part of man, his very soul that is the origin and author of all evil desires for worldly things. Take away the soul and no voluptuousness remains. St. Paul calls these things the wisdom of the flesh. But I would gladly know what he understands by unclean desires and by voluptuousness. Does he understand by them evil thoughts, adultery, fornication, man-slaughter, theft, covetousness, deceit, uncleanness, blasphemy, pride, and foolishness ?   These things come from the heart of man and are determined by the volition of the will as our Master Christ clearly says (Mark 7, 18-23).

These unclean desires come not from the bones nor from the sinews, but from the very bottom of the heart.   For all that is in man, heart, soul, flesh, and bone, with all their works is but flesh unless the Spirit of God be there.   Every man has a soul, but that does not make him Christ's for then infidels would be Christians.   It is the spirit of Christ that makes him Christ's, and the Spirit of God bears witness to our spirit that we are the children of God.

Without the Spirit of God we are in sin, though our own spirit do the best it can, for they are not the children of God who are guided by their own spirit.   Our spirit can do no good at all, only evil.   But now damnable reason and fleshly wisdom will dispute and say that if our free will can do no good then why does God command so many good things ?   Why did God give commandments which are impossible for us to keep ?   And, if it is impossible for us to keep them, what right does God have to damn us for failing in those things which it is impossible to do ?

Where has blind, presumptuous, and damnable reason learned to enquire about the Maker's will or to murmur against the ordinances of the living God ?   Who are you to require an explanation for His acts ?   He made you without your consent and counsel.   May He not establish laws and commandments to govern you at His pleasure and without your advice ?   You are not worthy of an answer : moreover you are so presumptuous that no godly answer will satisfy you.

First, you must grant that God is essential goodness and nothing but goodness.   Therefore He can command nothing but what is good, just, and righteous. The goodness of God is not nullified because you do not or cannot do that which is good because of your wickedness and your inability to do that which is good. If you are not able to do the good things He commands you, there is no fault in Him who commands or in the commandments themselves. Why then do you complain against Him without a cause and murmur, saying that He knows they are impossible for you to keep ? The truth is that He does know it. Then why, you ask, does He command them ? It is sufficiently answered to say that it is His pleasure to command as He does.

But I will go further. Your Maker knows that these commandments are impossible for you, and He knows your damnable and presumptuous pride who think that you can do well of your own strength and without any other help. It is to subdue your presumptuous pride and to bring you to a knowledge of yourself that He has given you His commandments. You cannot complain of them because they are both righteous and good. If you complain because they are impossible for you, then consider your damnable pride who thought yourselves so strong you could do all good things.

These commandments cannot and will not be changed to satisfy your presumptuous pride. Therefore, say what you will, they are God's ordinance which may not be changed. There is only one remedy and that is to confess your weakness, to confess your pride, to acknowledge your inability to keep them and to grant that these commandments are lawful, holy, and good, and to laud and praise God for them. You can only go to your merciful God with this confession and to pray that He will help you, be merciful to you, strengthen you in your weakness, and give you His Spirit. Your spirit is too carnal to fulfil these spiritual commandments but doubt not that you will find Him merciful and gracious. He gave these commandments to make manifest your pride and weakness that you might seek Him and call upon Him for help.

The Pelagians thought they had made a great point when they reasoned that God would command nothing that was impossible. Bishop John Fisher and his scholars glory in this same reasoning to this very day. Augustine answers them by saying that everyone knows that God makes commandments which men cannot keep. He does this so we may know what we should pray for. Through faith, prayer obtains in us the things which the law commands. Through faith we obtain the strength to keep the commandments of the law. God moves and causes us to will what is good and gives us a good will. Without Him we should only will what is evil.

Here we should also note that the Pelagians and our scholastic theologians agree in saying that the grace of God helps man's good purpose so that man has a good intention and desire. Duns Scotus says that man disposes himself by attrition to receive grace and then God helps him. The truth is contrary to this for there is no good purpose in man, no good disposition, no good intent. Everything is opposed to goodness, and clean contrary to everything that agrees with grace until God of His mercy comes and gives grace and changes man's will to grace and gives him the will to desire what is good. And this God does when man has no thought of goodness and clearly resists all that is good.

Augustine says of the Pelagians that they grant that grace helps man's good purpose, but they do not say that God gives the love of virtue to him who strives against it. They speak as if man of himself, without the help of God, has a good purpose, and a mind to virtue, through which preceding merit he is worthy to be helped by the grace of God. Doubtless the grace that follows helps the good purpose of man, but there would never have been a good purpose if grace had not preceded. Though the good endeavour of man, where it begins, is helped by grace, yet did it never begin without grace.

Free will of its natural strength, without special grace, can do nothing but abide in sin. We may invent as many holy purposes as we will, as many subtle distinctions, as many good applications; they are all sin until grace comes. All that we can do is but hypocrisy and double sin until God chooses us. For, as He says, "You have not chosen me, but I have chosen you" (John 15, 16).

In the beginning God created man. These words refer to the creation of the first man. God left him in the hands of his own counsel. These words do not support free will but only signify that man was made lord over all inferior creatures to use them at his pleasure. This is clear from the second chapter of Genesis which tells how all creatures were brought before Adam to receive their names. They were all left to his use and his will, and he was lord over them all, and none over him. This was his kingdom in which he did reign and govern all things. This was by authority given him by God who added His commandments and precepts. In these words no power was given to Adam, he was given commandments whereby he was to be ordered and ruled. He was to rule not by his own counsel, but according to the commandments and counsels of God. By these commandments his freedom was limited as when God commanded him that he should not eat of the tree of knowledge of good and evil What power Adam had by his free will to keep this commandment, the fall of man has made plain.

The commandments declare the things that we ought to do. They also show our weakness so that we might learn to seek for a greater strength and help than is within us. It is plain that the commandments of God give us no strength, and they declare that there is no strength in us. They show us our duty and our weakness and move us to seek further for strength. As the words of the law threaten an evil end for sin only to dissuade evil doers and wicked persons from sin, so do the words of promise stir up and quicken good men's hearts to do well. They comfort them so that they do not despair in adversities.

Our Master Christ says: "How often would I have gathered your children and ye would not" (Matthew 23, 37). Here you ask, "If they had no free will, why did Christ say 'thou wouldst'?" First you must consider that there are two kinds of will in God. One is called His godly will, or His secret and inscrutable will, through which all things are ordered and done. No one has knowledge of this will so that he knows what to do or what not to do, for it is inscrutable and, therefore, it is sufficient for us to know that there is an inscrutable will. The other will in God is called His declared and manifest will which is given to us in holy Scripture. Men are bound to search and know this will and for that reason it was given to us. This will declares what every man is bound to do and what every man is bound to avoid. In accordance with this will salvation is offered to us, and by this will God will have no man damned, for He lets His Word be preached impartially to all men.

He that will know this will must go to our Master Christ in whom is the whole treasure of wisdom and knowledge. He will show us what it is necessary for us to know, and as much as our Father in heaven would have us know. The Scripture speaks of God who was incarnate, who was sent to will, to speak, to do, to preach, to do miracles and to suffer death for our salvation.

Now He says, "I would have gathered thy children." That is to say: "I did preach, I did labour with all diligence to convert you, I did miracles before you, I wept and I wailed for your sake. All these things I did with everything that might convert you and with all that was determined for God Incarnate to do." But all these things did not profit them. Why ? Because they would not accept Him. There was no fault in Him. There was nothing left undone that belonged to His doing. He was willing, and yet it did not profit Jerusalem because they would not receive Him.

Why would they not ? Was it because they had the power to consent or not to consent ? No, but because as John says : " They could not believe because He had blinded their eyes and hardened their hearts so that they should not see with their eyes nor understand with their hearts " (John 12, 40). They could do no other thing of their wills but refuse to accept His preaching. The liberty of their will gave them power to be against Christ but not to accept Him. There was no power or intent in their wills to consent to Christ, but only to will the contrary because they were blinded and their hearts were hardened. Therefore, of their natural strength they could do no other than turn from Christ. Why were they blinded and why were their hearts hardened ? That you must enquire of the inscrutable will of God. The cause thereof I am sure He could answer you if He would. I am sure it is righteously done. That is enough for me.

But now comes blind and selfish reason and murmurs at this and asks why we are condemned and why God punishes us when we can do nothing but sin. He blinds us, He makes our hearts hard, and we cannot amend ourselves of our own will. Why does He complain against us and lay our offences to our charge ? Nothing is done but by His will, and we are but the instruments of His will. And, if we do not well, why does He not give us strength to do better ?

Why do you murmur against God ? You must grant that God, your Maker and the Governor of all things, is most wise, righteous, and merciful. He is so wise that nothing that He does can be improved, so righteous that there can

be no suspicion of unrighteousness in Him, so merciful that
He can do nothing without mercy.   If you grant that He does
all things righteously then you must grant that you have
suffered no wrong.   If you grant that He does all things
mercifully, then you must confess that in your blindness and
hardness of heart He has treated you better than you deserve.
You believe that God is righteous, wise, and merciful.   Now
faith is of those things that do not appear and cannot be
proved by external causes.   Hold fast to this faith and all
fleshly reason will be set aside.   For when God saves so few
men and damns so many, and you know not the cause, you
must still believe that He is merciful and righteous.

You have no reason to complain, for you have suffered
no wrong.   You have everything that is yours, and nothing
has been taken from you that belongs to you.   Why do you
complain that He gives mercy to one and none to the other ?
I answer, what is that to you ?   Is not His mercy His own ?
Is it not lawful for Him to give to whom He will ?   Is your
eye evil because He is good ?   Take what is yours and go
your way (Matthew 20, 15).   For if it is His will to show His
wrath and to make His power known over the vessels of
wrath, ordained to damnation, and to declare the riches of His
glory to the vessels of mercy which He has prepared and
elected to glory, what is that to you (Romans 9, 23) ?   What
cause do you have to complain ?   It is the will of God which
can only be good and righteous.

Therefore put an end to your murmuring and disputation
against God and believe that He is, of nature, merciful and
takes no delight or pleasure in your damnation.   Believe steadfastly that if He shows His mercy to only one man in all the
world that you shall be that same one man.   Though an
angel would make you believe that all the world shall be
damned, yet stick fast to His mercy and to His justice that
justifies you, and believe that the sweet blood of His blessed

Son cannot be shed in vain. Believe that it must justify sinners, as many as stick fast to it, though they be ever so blinded and ever so hardened, for it was shed only for them.

Our theologians have sought to discover the cause of predestination and reprobation. Duns Scotus, halting between carnal reason and the invincible Scriptures of St. Paul, cannot tell whether the will of God is alone the cause of election or whether the merits of man preceding election are an efficient cause, and concludes that both opinions may be defended. Bonaventure blindly concludes that there may be a cause preceding election to deserve it. In these unfruitful questions which engender nothing but contention they have spent all their lives. For these things they are given such peculiar names as the "subtle", "seraphical", and "irrefragible" doctors. Against them all I set St. Paul who took great labour to prove by invincible Scriptures and examples thereof that there was no other cause, but only the will of God. To prove this he submitted the evident example of Jacob and Esau which tells how Jacob was elected and Esau reproved before they were born, and before they had done good or bad. Can there be a plainer example ?

But here blindness will say that God foresaw that Jacob should do good, and therefore He chose him. He saw also that Esau would do no good and therefore He repelled him. Alas for blindness. How can you judge of what God saw ? How do we know that God saw that ? And if He saw it, how do we know that was the cause of Jacob's election ? These children are unborn, they have done neither good nor bad, and yet one of them is chosen and the other refused. St. Paul knows no other cause but the will of God.

And where you say that God did foresee that one of them would do good, I pray you what was the cause that made Jacob do good ? You must say that it was because God gave him grace to do good. Thus the will of God is still the cause

of election because God would give him the grace to do
good.   God saw that Jacob would do good, but so would
Esau also have done good if God would have given him that
same grace.

Therefore, be content with the will of God and doubt not
that the will of God is a righteous and lawful cause of
election.   St. Paul concludes the matter with these words
from Scripture : " I will show mercy to whom I show mercy :
I will have compassion on whom I have compassion " (Romans
9, 15).   It is plain that the reason why God elected us is not
because He saw before that we should do good.   The only
cause of election is His mercy, and the cause of our doing
good is His election.

If you believed that God was good, righteous, and merciful, it would be a great comfort to you that the election
stands only in His will.   Then you would be sure it would be
both righteously and mercifully done.   But you have no faith.
Therefore, you must needs mistrust God and fall to inventing
reasons of your own strength for election.   It is as if you
would say that because God of His righteousness and mercy
will not choose us, therefore we must make sure some other
way that we are elected.   First we will invent the idea that
election comes of deserving and then we will imagine certain
works that are appointed to us, and these we will do at our
pleasure, so that the election and reprobation shall stand in
our own hands, let God do what pleases Him.

Now because there are clear places in Scripture that give
to God alone the election and reprobation of sinners, therefore these men are troubled and can find no other remedy
but to study how they may wring and wrest the open Scriptures to satisfy their errors and their carnal reason.   Where
the Holy Ghost says : " I will harden the heart of Pharaoh ",
they take upon themselves to teach the Holy Ghost to speak
better and to say : " I will suffer Pharaoh to harden his heart,

but I will not do it." Contrary to this, Moses and Paul speak plainly and the Scriptures say that God hardened Pharaoh's heart. He did not harden his own heart.

You must grant that after the fall of Adam the pure nature of man was corrupted by sin, through which we are all wicked and born by nature the children of wrath. As David says, "We are all conceived in sin". Notwithstanding this corrupt nature, God makes all men both good and bad. Those that are good are good by His grace. Those that are bad are bad of corrupted nature, and yet God has made them. God works good, and evil works evil and He uses them both as instruments. Yet God does nothing evil. Evil is done only by an evil man. Take an example. A man saws a block with a dull saw. It is not in condition to cut effectively, yet at the motion of the man, it cuts even though it is dull. The action of the man in sawing is effectively done, but the saw cuts according to the nature of its dullness. So God moves evil human instruments to work, and by His influence given to all creatures, does not suffer them to be idle, but He does not change their nature. Therefore, their works are the appropriate fruit of their corrupted nature, but there is no fault in God's working in them.

Thus we see how God works in all men, both good and bad. But now let us look at the hardening of those that are evil. First they are evil by nature and can abide nothing that is good, nor suffer good to be done. Therefore, when God, the Author of goodness, does anything or says anything to them they turn more and more contrary to God and to all His works. Of their nature they are so corrupted that they cannot agree to the will of God nor to anything that is good. When such things are offered them, they blaspheme and withstand with all their might and power. They become provoked by their might and power. They become provoked by their corrupted nature to more mischief. For example, when the blessed Word of God is preached to them who are wicked and to whom God has not given the grace to receive it, they are not amended, but become more and more hardened. The more the Word of God is preached, the more obstinate they are and the more mischief they intend.

This is plainly seen in the corrupt nature of man. The more a thing is forbidden him, the more he desires to do it. But what need have we to go to Egypt to prove this ? Look at my own countrymen to see if they are not openly hardened and so blinded that no one is able to answer them by any reason or law. Therefore, they take themselves to violence and oppression as Pharaoh did. These are the signs and tokens of a hardened heart. For the more the Word of God and the very truth is declared to them, the more sturdy and obstinate they become against it. All their study, all their wits, all their counsels, all their craft, is employed to keep the Word of God under and to withstand the truth. They might rather give thanks to God and with great meekness and a humble spirit receive the heavenly truth.

5

HOLY SCRIPTURES*

It is lawful for all men to read Holy Scripture

*Most gracious Lord, of Thy mercy and grace I
beseech Thee, that I may have the strength to
defend Thy godly Word to Thy glory and honour,
and to the utter confusion of Thy mortal enemies.
Help good Lord, help, and I shall not fear a
thousand of Thine enemies. In Thy name will I
begin to defend this cause.*

THY faithful servant Moses, true and just in all Thy
works, commands faithfully and truly, and with great
earnestness, that man, woman, and child should diligently
read Thy holy Word. He says : " Set your hearts on all my
words which I testify unto you this day, that you may
command them to your children to keep, to do, and to fulfil
all things that are written in the book of this law " (Deuter-
onomy 32, 46). Mark how he commands them to teach
their children all things that are written in this book, and to
teach them that they might keep and fulfil them. Moses
made no secret of God's Word, for how can men fulfil words
and commands that they do not know ? How can men know
the true way of God if they do not have His Word ?

* *See note on page 106*

The psalmist says : " Thy word is a lantern unto my feet and a light unto my path " (Psalm 119, 105). He calls it a lantern and a light to all men. God's Word also says : " Blessed is the man whose delight is in the will of God and whose meditation is in God's law night and day " (Psalm 1, 2). Here the Spirit of God says that men who study the Word of God are blessed.

St. Paul commands us to receive the helmet of salvation and the sword of the spirit which is the Word of God (Ephesians 6, 17). Does he speak only to priests ? No, this epistle was written to the whole church of the Ephesians. They read it, and were they not laymen ? St. Paul calls it the sword of the spirit and is it not lawful for laymen to have the Spirit of God ? St. John says : " If any man come to you and bring not this doctrine receive him not into your house nor yet salute him " (2 John 10). Here the Holy Ghost wills that we should have no other doctrine but holy Scripture. Further, these words were written to a woman and her children.

Christ said to the Pharisees : " Search the scriptures, for in them you think to have eternal life " (John 5, 39). Our Master Christ sent the Pharisees to the Scriptures. Will you forbid Christians to read them ? St. Paul says : " All Scripture is given by inspiration of God which is profitable to teach, to improve, to inform, to instruct in righteousness, that the man of God may be perfect, and prepared unto all good works " (2 Timothy 3, 16-17). In the same Epistle, St. Paul says that Timothy was taught in holy Scriptures from his childhood, and that in them he was instructed unto salvation through faith in Christ Jesus.

Christ commanded His disciples to preach the Gospel to all creatures and teach men to keep the commandments He had given them. Mark that the Gospel must be preached to all kinds of men and not only to priests. You will say that you preach the Gospel to the people and that is enough. They need not have it in an English translation. But if they may hear it of you, why may they not also read it ? The nobles of Thessalonika who received the Word searched the Scriptures daily to see whether those things that Paul preached were true or not. Here you see that laymen searched the Scriptures to see whether St. Paul's preaching was true or not. How can you say that laymen shall not read the Scriptures but only receive them from your preaching ?

Priscilla and Aquila expounded the Scriptures to Apollo, a learned man. These were lay persons, and yet they were so learned in the Scriptures that they were able to teach a great doctor. The eunuch who was the treasurer of the Queen of the Ethiopians read the prophet Isaiah. He did not understand it until God sent him Philip to explain it to him. The eunuch was a layman, and also an infidel, and yet he was not forbidden by God to read the Scriptures but rather was helped to an understanding of them.

St. Paul says : " Let the Word of God dwell in you plenteously " (Colossians 3, 16). St. Paul would have laymen learn the Word of God, and that plenteously. Athanasius also said : " If you would have your children obedient to you, accustom them to the Word of God." You shall not say that study of the holy Scriptures belongs only to religious men. It belongs to every Christian, and especially to him that is wrapped in the business of this world, for he has more need of help because he is wrapped in the troubles of this world. Therefore, it is greatly to your profit that your children should both hear and read the Scriptures because there they will learn the commandment : Honour thy father and thy mother. Chrysostom also said : " I beseech you that you will often come hither and that you will diligently hear the lesson of holy Scripture, and not only when you are here.

When you are at home take in your hands the Bible and receive it with careful study for thereby you will have great advantage."

St. Jerome declared that, " If there is anything in this life that preserves a wise man and helps him to bear the oppressions and bondage of the world, I do reckon that it is the meditation and study of holy Scripture."

St. Paul says : " The Gospel is declared openly through preaching " (Titus 1, 3).   In another place he says : " God has brought life and immortality to light through the Gospel " (2 Timothy 1, 10).   Our Master calls it " the light of the world " (John 8, 12).   Now who will set a light under a bushel ?   Will he not place the light in the open so all men there may be lighted ?   The Gospel is given to be proclaimed and everyone is bound to accept it.   Therefore, it must be proclaimed to every man.

6

TEMPORAL AND RELIGIOUS AUTHORITY*

That men's constitutions, which are not grounded in Scripture, bind not the conscience of man under the pain of deadly sin.

IN this article we must note that there are two kinds of authorities and powers. One is a temporal power, the other is called a spiritual power. God has committed the temporal power to kings, dukes, earls, lords, barons, judges, mayors, sheriffs, and to all other ministers under them. These have only the temporal sword. Through it they regulate the commonwealth with all the worldly affairs pertaining to it.

St. Paul declares : " Let every soul be subject and obedient to the high powers " (Romans 13, 1). St. Peter also says : " Be subject unto the king as unto the chief head, either unto rulers as unto them that are of the king for the punishment of evil doers " (1 Peter 2, 13-14). We must be obedient to this power in all things that pertain to the ministration of this present life and of the commonwealth, not only (as Paul says) for avoiding punishment, but also for conscience' sake, for this is the will of God. It this power tyrannically makes any command contrary to right and law, our charity must suffer it, provided it is not repugnant to the Gospel or

* See note on page 108

destructive of faith.   For, as St. Paul says, " Charity suffers
all things " (1 Corinthians 13, 7).   Our Master Christ also
says: " If a man strike thee on one cheek, turn him the
other " (Matthew 5, 39).   If he commands you anything
contrary to justice, or does you any wrong, you may resist with
a good conscience, if you can do so through reasonable means,
without sedition, insurrection, or disruption of the peace.   If
you can avoid an unjust imprisonment without being guilty
of a seditious act, you may lawfully do so, but in no case
may you resist with sword or hand, but you must obey.

We have many examples in Scripture to show that men
have fled from the tyranny of unjust power.   Elisha fled
from the tyranny of the King of Syria (2 Kings 6), Peter fled
from prison (Acts 12), and St. Paul fled from the city of
Damascus (Acts 9) and out of Iconium (Acts 14).   You may
not offer physical resistance, but you may only flee or else
obey the thing that is commanded you.   If it is right and
to the profit of the commonwealth, you must accept your
penalty and abide where you are.

It will be asked whether we would be bound to obey the
king's command if it should please his grace to condemn the
New Testament in English and to forbid his subjects to have
it at his displeasure.

To this I will answer that I do not believe that our most
noble prince has forbidden Christians to have Christ's
Testament whether it be in Latin, English, French, German,
Greek, or Hebrew, for Christ's truth is the same in all
languages.   It would be very unreasonable for anyone to
forbid the king to know or read his earthly father's will which
only promised worldly goods subject to decay and corruption.
If this would be unreasonable and wrong, how much more
would it not be wrong to take away from us the Testament
of our Father in heaven whose legacy and promises exceed the
earthly legacies of the father of the king as far as God excells

man ? But why should I give proofs to his grace that it is
lawful for us to possess what the Father of heaven has sent
us, from Whom comes nothing but goodness ? Yes, and this
legacy was not sent by man, or by an angel or saint, but
by the only Son of God and man who declared it to all the
world. He did not give it to the Pharisees alone, but to all
kinds of people and that to the very hour of death. He
finally died and still was not content, because He sent His
apostles to teach this Word through the world. Because the
ministry of this Word required a greater strength than is in
natural man, He gave them His eternal spirit to establish
them, to confirm them, and to make them strong in all
things so that nothing might be lacking for the declaration and
setting forth of His Word.

Now what true subject that regards the honour of our
noble prince and the salvation of his soul could think that
his grace would condemn that thing that comes from the
Father of heaven and was sent and taught by His eternal
Son, a thing which He sealed with His most precious blood ?
Who could think that the king would condemn that which
Christ commanded His glorious apostles to preach confirming
it with many miracles and with the authority of the Holy
Ghost ?

It is plain that the Father of heaven did not send this
godly Word with small diligence as though He did not care
whether it remained on earth or not. He has declared this
holy Word with such a process that heaven, earth, and hell
should know that it is His Word and His will, that all men
should have it, and that He would defend it and be the enemy
of all them that would oppose it. Let those who are enemies
of the king in spirit and in deed suspect that his grace would
oppose the Scriptures. I never will. I dare boldly say that
the devil in hell who is an enemy of his grace will tempt him

to condemn God's Word. This the king knows and I do not doubt but that he will avoid the danger.

Nevertheless it may please God to take vengeance for our abominable sins so that after the reign of his grace is ended, God may send us a tyrant as will not only forbid the New Testament, but also those things which are to the honour of God. Yes, and this may be done under such a pretence of God's name that men may imagine him a friend of God.

This will be a terrible scourge and an intolerable plague. May the Father in heaven defend us from such a terrible vengeance. It is the greatest plague that can come on earth, as St. Paul says to the Romans, when God's truth is condemned in God's name and men are so blind that they cannot perceive it. This plague never comes but as a token of everlasting reprobation. May our Redeemer, Christ Jesus, defend us from it.

But if we must suffer this plague, how shall Christians act toward a prince that condemns God's Word ? My lords, the bishops, would depose him with short deliberation and make no conscience of it. They have deposed princes for lesser causes than this by a great deal. Against them I will always submit Christ, His holy apostles, and the Word of God, which Christian men must follow. If the king forbids the New Testament or any of Christ's sacraments, the preaching of the Word of God, or commands anything against Christ under pain of punishment or death, men shall first make prayers to God, and then diligent intercession unto the king's grace with all due subjection that his grace would withdraw that commandment. If he will not do so, they shall keep their Testament with all other ordinances of Christ and, if they cannot flee, let the king exercise his tyranny. Under no circumstances shall they withstand him with violence but suffer patiently all the tyranny that he imposes on them both in their bodies and in their property. They must leave vengeance to their heavenly Father, Who has a scourge with which to tame those bedlams when His time comes.

In no wise shall they resist violently, neither shall they deny Christ's truth nor forsake it before the ruler lest they run in the danger of the words : " He that denieth me and my word before men, him shall I deny before my Father in heaven " (Matthew 10, 33). Let no one regard this matter lightly and think he may give up his Testaments and yet not deny Christ. Whoever gives up the Scriptures, as a thing worthy to be condemned, he denies Christ before God.

If a learned man finds any faulty translation or errors in printing in his Testament, he shall gladly amend that fault, but he should not permit the whole Testament to be condemned as unlawful because of faults in it. If that were permitted, we would have no New Testament, for there is none so true that it is beyond error or criticism. This I say boldly, that the New Testament in English is ten times more accurate than the old translation in Latin, in which whole sentences are lacking in many places, and there are other places that no one can depend on because they are evidently false. Yet we may not burn our books for all that, but keep them and amend them. Neither shall they depose their prince as my lords, the bishops, were wont to do. They shall boldly confess that they have the truth and will hold to it. They shall pray to their heavenly Father to change the heart of their ruler that they may live under him in accordance with Christ's Word in peace and quietness. St. Paul exhorts us, saying : " I exhort that prayers, supplications, petitions and giving of thanks be had for all men; for kings and for all that are in pre-eminence, that we may live a quiet and a peaceable life in all goodness and honesty " (1 Timothy 2, 12).

When the priests of the temple commanded Peter and John not to preach and teach in the name of Jesus, they answered that it was more right to obey God than man (Acts 4 & 5). The Pharisees also commanded our Master Christ in Herod's name that He should depart from thence or he would kill Him. He would not obey them but answered to Herod with a great threat : " Go tell the wolf, Behold I cast out devils and make men whole this day and tomorrow, and on the third day I am consumed. Nevertheless, I must continue this day, tomorrow, and the next day " (Luke 13, 32-33). Therefore He left not the ministration of the Word either for the king's pleasure nor yet for the fear of death.

We have also the three children who would not obey the commandment of Nebuchadnezzar because it was against the Word of God (Daniel 3). We have an example also where King Darius commanded that no one should make any petition either to God or man for the space of thirty days, but only to him, the king. Nevertheless Daniel went into his house and three times a day made his prayers to the God of Jerusalem. For this he was put into the den of lions, consenting to the punishment but not to the wrong commandment. Thus Christians are bound to obey in suffering the king's tyranny, but not in consenting to his unlawful commandment, always having in mind the comforting saying of Christ : " Fear not them that kill the body, which when they have done, they can do no more " (Matthew 10, 28). Likewise Peter says : " Happy are ye if ye suffer for righteousness' sake, nevertheless fear not, though they seem terrible to you, neither be troubled, but sanctify the Lord God in your heart " (1 Peter 3, 14-15). Let them not fear but that their Father in heaven cares for them and shall deliver them, and that He will bring His godly Word into light when it shall please His eternal will which no tyrant is able to withstand.

When the tyrants feel most sure of a victory then shall He appear to make Joseph, when he is sold in slavery in Egypt and cast in prison, the lord over all Egypt, and also over

The death and burning of the most constant Martyrs in Christ,
D. Rob. Barnes, Tho. Garret, and W. Hierome, in Smithfielde. an. 1541.

¶ A briefe difcourfe of the lyfe and doinges of Robert
Barnes Doctour in Diuinitie, a bleffed feruaunt and Martyr of Chrift, fummarely extracted out of the booke of *Monumentes.*

He firft bringing vp of the fayd Rob. Barnes
from a childe, was in the vniuerfitie of Cambridge,
and was made a Nouice in ye houfe of ye Fryer Auguftines there. And beyng very apt vnto learning, did fo
profite, that by the helpe of his frendes, he was retho-
ned from thece to the vniuerfitie of Louayne in Bra-
bant, where he remained certayne yeares, and greatly profited in the ftudy of the tongues, and there pro-
ceded Doctour of Diuinitie. And then from thence
returned agayne into England, and fo to the vniuerfitie of Cambridge, where he was made Prior and Mai-
fter of the houfe of Auguftines, wherein he was firft
brought vp. And at that tyme the knowledge of good
letters was fcarcely entred into the vniuerfitie, all thynges being full of rudenes &
barbariette, fauing in very felne, which were pfupe and fecrete: whereupon Barnes
hauing fome feling of better learning, and had red better actours, begã in his houfe to
rrade Terence, Cicero, and Plautus, fo that what with his induftry, paynes and labours, and with the helpe of Thomas Parnell his fcholer, whom he brought from Lo-
uaine

A page from the Daye edition of the works of Dr. Barnes published
in 1572. The lower half of the page shows the beginning of the
biography of Barnes written by John Foxe.

them that sold him. He also brings to pass that Haman shall be hanged on his own gallows. When Pharaoh has commanded the destruction of all the children of Israel, God finds the means to save Moses, and all the power of Egypt cannot save the king.

Why should I bring many examples to demonstrate God's power and to show that God's truth and His children are always persecuted but their end is always glorious ? Therefore, this one example of our Master Christ shall be sufficient to establish and confirm feeble hearts, and also to soften stony hearts and, finally, to confound the violent tyranny of mortal tyrants who are but stubble, hay, and dust, and in a moment are brought to a lump of stinking carrion. Consider our Master Christ who is the very true Son of God, yea God Himself, and yet He is crucified and put to death as a seditious person, as a malefactor, as a thief, as a traitor, yea, and as an heretic. He is laid in a grave and a great stone placed before the door. Soldiers, not of the common sort, but Romans, are set diligently to keep the grave with all the subtlety and wisdom that the authorities could devise. And all this was done so He would not rise up according to His word. But all this did not help, the power of God could not be hindered, His truth could not be false, His Word could not be oppressed. When the tyrants thought to make their victorious triumph, then were they completely overcome. Neither water nor fire, sea nor land, heaven nor earth, death nor hell can prevent God from defending His children or bringing His Word to light, or keeping His eternal promises. Therefore, let Christians not fear to keep the Word of God, and hold fast to it and not deny it for any tyranny. The day shall be greatly to their glory. Sodom and Gomorrah shall be more lightly handled than such princes as persecute the holy Word of God.

But this article is not written against the temporal power. It is not concerned with the conscience, but only with the ordering of worldly things. Therefore, it ministers a temporal pain over the body only and therewith is content. Therefore, we will now speak of the power which men call spiritual.

First, it is to be noted that this is not a worldly authority or power, but only a ministration of the Word of God and a spiritual regiment. It is concerned with preaching, with the governing of the soul, and with the ministration of the spirit. It has nothing to do with the external justice and righteousness of the world, and, therefore, it has no power by right and law to make any statutes to order the world, but only to preach faithfully and truly and to minister the Word of God.

St. Paul, as he himself said, " durst speak no other thing but those things which Christ had wrought in him " (Romans 15, 18), and cursed anyone, man or angel, who should preach any other Gospel (Galatians 1, 8). The prophet commands us not to hear the words of those who deceive us, for they speak visions of their own, which are not out of the mouth of God, and yet they speak in the name of God. Therefore, they should only be heard so long as they speak the Word of God. Christ Himself says, " He that heareth you heareth me " (Luke 10,16), and " Whatsoever they say unto you sitting in the seat of Moses, do it " (Matthew 23, 3). By sitting in the seat of Moses is to be understood the teaching of God, and therefore God teaches through them. But if they teach their own doctrine we are not to hear it or do it, for such men seek what is theirs, and not Christ's.

These words are plain against them that preach anything but the Word of God. Therefore, if these men will make any laws or statutes above the Word of God they must be considered in two ways : first whether they be openly and directly against the Word of God and to the destruction of faith. This they have done in that statute whereby they have condemned the New Testament and forbidden certain men to preach the Word of God without having a true cause against them except their malicious suspicions. This they have done when they teach that works justify and in the statute whereby they bind men under the pain of damnation to be absolved by them. These statutes, I say, with others like them, men are not bound to obey, neither of charity nor to avoid scandal. The more men are offended by the Word of God and the stiffer they be against it, the more openly and plainly must we resist them, who make such laws, with the words : " We are more bound to obey God than men."

All traditions of men that are against God's law must be destroyed. Therefore let every man take heed. It will be no excuse for him to say that his guide was blind. Let them hear the Word of God and His prophets : " Walk not in the precepts of your fathers, and keep not their judgments, but walk in my precepts and keep my judgments " (Ezekiel 20, 18).

The second kind of statutes are those which command certain indifferent things as if they must be done of necessity and under pain of deadly sin. The eating of fish or flesh on this day or that, for example, is an indifferent thing and a matter of freedom. So it is also to wear raiment of this or that colour, to shave our heads or not, for a priest to wear a long or a short gown, a grey friar to wear grey or a russet coat, a white friar to wear white or black, a priest to marry or not, and whether a hermit shall wear a beard or not. These and all similar outward works are matters of indifference which may or may not be done. Now, if the bishops should make any law or statute that these things shall be done, by compulsion, so that it shall not be lawful for us to leave them undone but that we must do them precisely and not the contrary under pain of deadly sin, then we must oppose them and in no wise obey them. To obey them is to hurt our faith and the liberty of Christendom under which we are free and are not bound to any external work. We are free in all things and in every way except where brotherly charity or the common peace should be offended.

We are free in all these things and we must withstand those who would take this liberty from us with this text of Scripture : " We are bought with the price of Christ's blood, we shall not be the servants of men " (1 Corinthians 7, 23). This text is clearly against them who will bind the consciences of men to sin in those things in which Christ has left them free. Of this we have an evident example of St. Paul who would not circumcise Titus when the false brethren would have compelled him to it as a thing of necessity. St. Paul did not withstand them because circumcision was unlawful or was improper for Christians, but because they would have compelled him to it, as a thing of necessity. This St. Paul would not permit, because it was contrary to the liberty we have in Christ Jesus, as He says plainly. Therefore, Christ has not only made us free from sin, but He has also given us freedom in indifferent things. Therefore we cannot be bound to them as if they were things of necessity, like eating fish on Friday, and to be bound to it under pain of mortal sin. In such matters we may not be obedient because that would be contrary to the Word of God. This is not because it is evil to eat fish (for, in time convenient and when you are disposed to it, it is good) but because they will bind our consciences in this matter and make a thing of necessity what God has left free.

St. Paul speaks against them in these words : " In the latter days certain men shall swerve from the faith applying themselves to the spirit of errors and doctrines of the devil forbidding marriage, to abstain from meats that God has created to be received by faithful men with thanks : for all creatures of God are good, and nothing to be refused that

is received with thanks " (1 Timothy 4, 3-4). Mark how St.
Paul says that nothing is to be refused that may be received
with thanks.   He opposes them that will forbid either fish
or flesh this day or that day, as a thing improper for a
Christian to eat.   St. Paul says in another place : " Meat
doth not commend us to God " (1 Corinthians 8, 8),   and
" The kingdom of heaven is neither meat nor drink " (Romans
14, 17).   Therefore, they do ill to bind our consciences in
such things and to think us unfaithful because we do not
observe them.

St. Paul says : " We ought not to be led with the traditions
of men that say, Touch not, taste not, handle not, which
things perish with the using of them, and are after the
commandments and doctrine of men : which things have the
similitude of wisdom in superstitions, holiness, and humility
in that they spare not the body and do the flesh no worship
unto his need " (Colossians 2, 8 and 21-23).   Here the super-
stition and feigned holiness that men have invented in eating
and drinking, in touching or handling, is condemned, as if
we reckon ourselves holy when we do them or guilty of deadly
sin when we do not do them.   We are made free through
Christ and are not bound to anything men order unless it be
contained in holy Scripture.

Christ has made us free and nothing can bind us to the
censure of sin but His Word.   It is clear that if any power
commands anything contrary to God's Word, or to the
destruction or diminution of the same, no one may obey
it under pain of damnation.   Nevertheless, if any of
these things are recommended, as things indifferent, we shall
keep them in time and place convenient where we may serve
a brother or edify him or do him good or possibly bring him
to the truth.   Yet at another time or place where I shall
not offend my brother, engender scandal or disquiet in the

commonwealth, I may freely, without any charge of conscience, or sin, break the commandment.

To eat flesh on Friday is forbidden by the bishops. Now,
if they compel you to it as a thing necessary and without
which you cannot be saved, then you must not obey, under
pain of sin. But if they will have you keep this as something
that may be an external means to mortify the body or to give
an outward appearance of holiness, and compel you to it by
an outward discipline, you may obey out of charity so as
not to break an outward order or cause disquiet for the sake
of things that neither make you good nor condemn you before
God. For, as St. Paul says : " If we eat neither are we the
better, nor if we eat not are we the worse " (1 Corinthians
8, 8), always provided you do not place your confidence in
these indifferent things nor yet offend your brother in them.
Though you are free in yourself and the matter may be indifferent, yet out of love you make yourself the servant of all
men. St. Paul says : " When I was free from all things yet
I did make myself a servant that I might win many men "
(1 Corinthians 9, 19). Note that he always speaks of weak
brethren, and not of obstinate and obdurate persons against
whom you must always withstand and defend your liberty.
That person is a weak brother who has a good mind and
believes the Word of God, but yet does not have the gift
to perceive the liberty to use indifferent things freely and
with thanks. Therefore, faith and charity must be your
guide in all these things. Following them you cannot err.

APPENDIX

Notes on the published works of Robert Barnes

A. THE SENTENCES

THE first published work of Robert Barnes was his *Sentences,* written in Latin and published under the title, *Sententiae ex Doctoribus Collectae, Quas Papistae Valde Impudenter Hodie Damnant.* It was printed by Johannes Klug at Wittenberg in 1530 under Barnes' pseudonym during exile, *Antonius Anglus* of Wittenberg. It was a 152-page octavo with a preface by John Bugenhagen, one of the reformers in the Lutheran circle at Wittenberg. A German translation was published the following year under the title *Fuernehmlich Artickel, Neulich Verteuscht, Von Dr. Antonius Aus England.* Bugenhagen was the translator. This work might best be described as a debaters' manual. It dealt with eighteen articles of religion which Barnes supported by quotations from the Bible and from the church fathers. The last item is an historical survey of the development of the Mass. In this work Barnes is revealed as an apt disciple of the Lutheran reformers, as well as a well-informed student of holy Scripture and the church fathers. It is especially noteworthy that the nineteen articles have a close correspondence to the Augsburg Confession which was also published in 1530. The *Sentences* were never published in English, but the high regard in which the work was held by the Lutherans is evident from the fact that a German translation of the original Latin was published in two editions in 1531.

The preface indicates that Barnes was living in Bugen-hagen's home in the summer of 1530 when the book was written. Bugenhagen refers to Barnes as a "faithful and learned theologian". The nineteen titles in Barnes' manual follow :

1. Faith alone justifies.
2. The death of Christ has sufficed for all sins, not only for original sin.
3. The law of God cannot be kept by our ability.
4. By its own strength free will can only sin.
5. The righteous sin in all good works.
6. What the true church is and how one may recognize it.
7. The keys of the church are God's Word, not the power of men.
8. Councils may err.
9. Everyone shall receive the Sacrament in both kinds.
10. Priests may take wives in marriage.
11. Human decrees cannot bind men in sin.
12. Auricular confession is not necessary for salvation.
13. Monks are not more holy than laymen because of their cowls or their cloisters.
14. Christian fasting does not stand in discrimination in foods.
15. For a Christian every day is a sabbath or holy day, and not only the seventh day.
16. Unjust excommunication by the pope does not harm the excommunicated.
17. In the Sacrament of the Altar is the true body of Christ.
18. Saints should not be called on as mediators.
19. Of the origin of the Mass

B. THE SUPPLICATION

By far the most important of the literary works of Robert Barnes, *The Supplication* was written in English and addressed to Henry VIII. Simon Cock printed it at Antwerp in 1531. The full title was : A supplication made by Robert Barnes doctour in divinity unto the most excellent and redoubted prince king henrye the eight.

A second edition was printed in London by J. Bydell in 1534. It had three new esays, but omitted six that were in the first edition. This edition has a woodcut, unidentified by any caption, which must be assumed to be Dr. Barnes. Its striking similarity to a well-known woodcut of Erasmus is curious. Another edition was published by H. Syngleton in London, possibly in the year 1555. It includes the same items as the Bydell edition, but docs not have the woodcut of Barnes.

The definitive edition of the works of Robert Barnes was produced by John Foxe and printed by Daye in London in 1572. Foxe collated the essays of the preceding editions and included them all in a monumental volume containing the works of Tyndale, Frith, and Barnes. The section devoted to the essays of Barnes was preceded by a biography extracted from the *Acts and Monuments,* the well-known history of martyrdom published by John Foxe during the reign of Elizabeth I. The title page of the *Works of Tyndale, Frith, and Barnes* referred to them as " three worthy martyrs, and principal teachers of this church of England." The preface spoke of them as " three fathers of blessed memory, chief ringleaders in these latter times of this church of England." John Foxe said that these men " in one cause, and about one time sustained the first brunt, in this our latter age, and gave the first onset against the enemies." Foxe expressed his gratitude " for the special gifts of fruitful erudition and plentiful knowledge wrought in them by God, and so by them left unto us in their writings."

Since that time only two publications have reprinted portions of the writings of Robert Barnes. The first of these was one volume of a series titled *Fathers of the English Church,* edited by L. Richmond. Volume I included the lives and portions of the works of Tyndale, Frith, Hamilton, Joy, and Barnes. It was published in London in 1807 and dedicated to George III. It includes the life of Barnes extracted from the *Acts and Monuments* of John Foxe, Winchester's (Stephen Gardiner) *Articles Against Barnes,* George Joy's *Refutation* and Barnes' essays on *Justification* and *Free Will.*

The second nineteenth century publication to recall the life and work of Barnes was published in 1830 by the Religious Tract Society of London. The title is *Writings of Tyndale, Frith, and Barnes.* It included a translation of the titles of Barnes' Latin *Sentences,* and the essay on *Justification.*

Barnes was prompted to write *The Supplication* because of far-reaching changes that had taken place in England since his flight to Germany in 1528. By 1530 Henry decided to marry the Protestant Anne Boleyn and Parliament had begun the legislation that was to break the relationships between the papacy and the church in England. By 1530 the Lutheran princes had demonstrated their political solidarity at the Diet of Augsburg where they had stated their faith in the Augsburg Confession. Late in 1530 they organized themselves in the Schmalkaldic League and invited the King of England to join them. Henry VIII responded that:

he was to his great satisfaction informed by them, that their great aim and design was to heal the distempers of the Church, and procure a reformation of those things, which either through the naughtiness or ignorance of men had been depraved and corrupted, without doing any injury to religion or disturbing the public peace.

Those physicians, therefore, deserve the greatest applause who so apply their medicines as to heal the wound, or cure the disease, without exasperating the parts; and he does not doubt but their endeavours have such a tendency as this.

And since they make mention in their letters of the reverence due to magistrates, he therefore gives them this short advice, that they would not open a gap to any licentiousness this way; and if they use but a sufficient caution at this point, their endeavours after a reformation will prove a kindness of the highest import to the public.

The Supplication of Robert Barnes to Henry VIII was intended to demonstrate Barnes' personal loyalty to his king and to show that the Lutheran Reformation was compatible both with the sovereignty of the English monarchy and the kind of reformation that Henry desired for England.

As a result of the ideas expressed in his book, Barnes was invited to return to England. One copy of the book had been sent to the king, another to the chancellor, Sir Thomas More. Barnes had an interview with the king and soon after was made King's Chaplain and an official representative of the government in the Anglo-Lutheran diplomacy in the 1530's. Sir Thomas More made a fruitless effort to bring Barnes to trial as a relapsed heretic.

1.   *A Supplication Unto The Most Gracious Prince King Henry the Eighth.*

Barnes' book has been identified by the title of the first one of the essays included in it.   There are two versions of this essay. The first version is found only in the Antwerp edition of 1531. Later editions included the second version which was written after Henry VIII had assumed the role of head of the English Church. Basically, the first version is an academic discussion of the separation of church and state. In it Barnes elaborated on the functions of the spiritual and temporal swords. He denied the clergy any temporal authority and said that their function was only the ministration of God's Word. He said that the spiritual sword was ordained to quicken, not to kill, and said that Christ Jesus, the mediator between God and man " has divided the offices of both powers into their proper acts and distinct dignities. Christian emperors, as concerning eternal life, have need of bishops, and likewise the bishops . . . need the emperor's laws." Addressing himself directly to the king, Barnes said that " your grace must have full power over all worldly affairs and bishops only the ministration of the Word of God. As your grace may not usurp to preach the Word of God, no more may they usurp any power that belongs to your sword."

When Henry VIII renounced papal authority in England and was acknowledged the head of the church, the limitations which Barnes had imposed on the state in reference to spiritual matters were unacceptable and Barnes' second essay was drastically rewritten. In place of a discussion of the proper separation of church and state, Barnes wrote a vehement attack on the clergy with numerous historical examples of the usurpation of temporal authority by bishops and popes. The second essay was much less personal than the first and appealed less in behalf of Barnes' own plight and the injustice done to him than to the menace of the oaths of the bishops which threatened the sovereignty and the integrity of the English monarchy. When the second edition of this essay was published in 1534, it was much safer to attack the clergy than to limit the king's power in matters of religion.

Both essays were perfectly clear in demonstrating the loyalty of Barnes to Henry VIII and in showing that Lutheranism was not a threat to the English monarchy.

2. *The Cause of My Condemnation.*

Barnes here enumerates the twenty-five charges that had been made against him as a result of his Christmas Eve sermon at Cambridge in 1525. The charges include the accusation that, though the preacher urged faithful prayers he had neglected to pray at the beginning of his sermon, had failed to pray for " our Lady ", for souls in purgatory, for the three estates of the church, and had criticized over-emphasis of observance of religious holidays. Barnes, the charges stated, had evidenced something less than a wholesome attitude toward the seriousness of heresy by denying his own guilt and responding, when asked whether he considered the men executed for heresy at Brussels to have been martyrs, that it seemed to him that anyone who died for the sake of God's Word was a martyr.

One of the charges against him came very near to Ana-baptism. He had criticized the litigiousness of the age, and, as a result, was accused of denying the propriety of taking legal matters to court at all. This section was re-edited in the second version of this essay. Only one of the alleged heresies seems to be Lutheran in its character. It was the twenty-fourth article which said that " men ought not to plead their own merit before Christ ", a view that suggests some knowledge and acceptance of the Lutheran doctrine of justification and good works.

Eighteen of the twenty-five articles were related to the ecclesiastical hierarchy, its corrupting wealth, and its unevan-gelical ostentation. Barnes realized that it was these matters that had brought him before the Cardinal, for he wrote later

that " I am sure that these words made me an heretic, for if
these words had not been therein, mine adversaries durst never
have shown their faces against me."

3. The Whole Disputation Between the Bishops and Dr. Barnes.

This essay was not in the edition of *The Supplication*
published in Antwerp in 1531. A growing anti-clericalism
in England made Barnes grasp the opportunity of demonstrating the judicial procedure and the religious attitudes
that had brought about his condemnation in 1526. He
recalled that both in his preliminary trial at Cambridge and
in the final trial at Westminster no specific charge of heresy
was laid against him, and that he was required to submit to
the authority of the church and read a revocation that was
prepared by his adversaries. He pleaded to the King, " I
beseech your highness to be good and gracious to me and
judge if this be charitable dealing thus to condemn me for an
heretic and not to show me the point therefore. But even
with a violent tyranny to compel me to do and confess what
they will or else be put to death."

That Barnes was not a Lutheran until his Wittenberg
days is clear from this essay in which he says that on the day
of his penance at St. Paul's, " The Bishop of Rochester (John
Fisher) must preach there the same day, and all his sermon
was against the Lutherians (*sic*) as though they had convicted
me for one."

All three of the first essays in *The Supplication* are written
in a vein of injured petulance that could hardly have made a
good impression on Henry VIII. They contain numerous
pleas like the following : " I beseech your grace of gracious
audience and of favourable justice. This thing I trust your
grace will not deny me, nor yet take any displeasure with

me your poor subject, for this requiring. For I have none
other prince nor lord to seek unto here on earth but your
grace only . . . I am compelled by extreme violence thus to
complain to your grace for my name, my fame, and my
estimation, and all things that belong to an honest poor man
in this world is taken wrongfully from me hereby, and have
been for the space of nine or ten years (which is no small
time) compelled to live in misery and obloquy."

4. *Onely Fayth Justifieth Before God.*

The Antwerp edition of this essay has an introductory
section dealing with ancient authorities and with the Anti-
christ which was omitted in later editions. Pleading the
authority of Scripture he says : " It is not right to bind us
always to the judgment of our old fathers, for then what need
have we of the gift of wisdom, what need have we of the gift
of understanding ? "   Warning against the Anti-christ he
said, " he shall be in all ages and without doubt he shall not
be a person despised in the world. He will not be a fool and
will not be unlearned, nor without the colour of holiness nor
without the name of a father, nor, in man's judgment, without
a good spirit."   Barnes then went on to say that the Anti-
christ will " preach Christ and also deny Christ, and will deny
Him with such subtlety that unless we stick fast to holy
Scripture and have the Spirit of God, we shall not recognize
him.   Therefore, let us now prove his spirit and we shall
soon see that he is not of God.   But first we must declare and
perfectly know what Christ is."

Another interesting omission in later editions is a depre-
cating reference to the title, *Defender of the Faith,* which
Henry VIII had received from the pope through the efforts
of Cardinal Wolsey and Bishop Clark. Both of these men
had been involved in Barnes' trial at Westminster in 1526.

Barnes closed his essay on justification with this gratuitous comment: "Now most excellent and gracious prince, it is not unknown to all the world that my lords the bishops have purchased your grace this title to be *Defender of the Faith*. Our Lord strengthen your grace that you may perform it even though none of the bishops would take great pains to declare, for your sake, what the true faith was that you were bound to defend. They left your grace as a man shut in a dark house that would fain come out but he could not find the door for want of light . . . Therefore, most noble prince . . . I have taken the labours and pains . . . to declare this article so plainly and strongly . . . that no faithful man can have any occasion to doubt it . . . " It is not difficult to see the reasons for deleting this section from later editions. It is also a vivid commentary on Barnes' lack of tact and an explanation of the king's aversion to him.

About one half of this essay by Barnes has been reproduced on pages 20-36. Repetitious material and duplications of illustrative examples have been omitted. An opening section in which the bishops are charged with being Anti-christ and numerous citations from the church fathers have also been left out.

5. *What the Church is and who be thereof, and whereby men may know her.*

This essay was included in the Antwerp edition of *The Supplication*. The Bydell and Syngleton editions substituted Barnes' response to Sir Thomas More's polemic against the first essay. The first essay is a comprehensive exposition of the doctrine of the church. It is reproduced almost in its entirety on pages 37 to 52.

6. *Another Declaration of The Church, Wherein He Answereth Master More.*

The most able defender of Roman Catholic theology in

England during the reign of Henry VIII was the lawyer, Sir Thomas More. He was Chancellor of England after the fall of Thomas Wolsey and was confronted with the problem of dealing with heretical literature written by English exiles abroad. Tyndale, Frith, and Barnes were the expatriates who troubled him most. A large part of his printed works are essays challenging the theology of the reformers. It was not the doctrine of justification but the Lutheran doctrine of the church that seemed the most menacing because he believed that Barnes was threatening the whole foundation of society in his first essay on the church.

Barnes had defined the church as a communion of saints, the whole number of believers on earth. He denied that the hierarchy of priests was the church, or that it consisted in any formal and outward structure. More could no more see the reality of an invisible church made up of an unidentifiable body of believers than Zwingli could grasp the reality of the body and blood of Christ in the Sacrament.

More believed that spiritual certainty was dependent on possession of a divinely appointed religious organism to define theology and speak with infallible authority. He rejected out of hand the view of Barnes that the true church may be known to exist "where the Word of God is purely and sincerely preached, and the Sacraments orderly administered after the blessed ordinance of Christ."

More twitted Barnes on what he called a careless use of sources and challenged his statements about the Epistle of James. He responded to Barnes' charge that some priests were living immoral lives by referring to the whoredom of the Protestant marriage of priests.

Barnes did not enter into a discussion of these issues but answered More's charges briefly and then simply repeated most of the matter of his first essay on the church. His major contention was that "The church is not a fellowship

gathered together in a consent of exterior things or cere-
monies. It is a fellowship specially gathered in a unity of
faith, having the Holy Ghost within them to sanctify their
spirits, which doth set their trust only in the redemption
promised them in Christ's blessed blood. This I say is the
very true church of God." Barnes' second essay on the
church is not reproduced in this volume because it is largely
a repetition of the first essay.

7. *What The Keys of The Church Be, And To Whom
They Were Given.*

A few repetitious passages and some citations from the
church fathers have been omitted. A long section charging
the clergy with fraud and venality in claiming exclusive
authority over the keys of the church is likewise not included.
Angrily Barnes wrote : " You make more laws and more
statutes, and dispense them for money, and all these things
you do by the authority of the keys that both open heaven
and hell and a man's coffer and also his purse."

About two thirds of Barnes' essay is reproduced on pages
53 to 61. This essay was omitted from the editions of
The Supplication printed by Bydell and Syngleton.

8. *Freewill of Man, After The Fall of Adam, Of His Natural
Strength, Can Do Nothing But Sin Afore God.*

This essay was slightly revised after its publication in the
Antwerp edition and was included in the Bydell and Syngleton
editions. It is essentially a treatise on the total depravity of
man, the grace of God, and the doctrine of election. The
edited essay on pages 62 to 76 is a little over half the
length of the original.

9. *That It Is Lawful For All Manner of Men To Read Holy Scripture.*

Only a small portion of this essay is reproduced on pages 77 to 80. Much of the original is an angry diatribe against the bishops for their failure to make an English Bible available to their people. Barnes introduced his essay by asking :

> How can Anti-christ be better known than by this token, that he condemneth Scriptures, and maketh it heresy and high treason against the King's grace for lay men to read Holy Scripture.

> Tell me what can be more contrary to Christ, than by violence to oppress the Scriptures, and to condemn them as unlawful, yea, and as heresie, for certain men to read, and to say that there be certain secrets in them that belong not for laymen to know ?

Barnes' attack was primarily turned toward Tunstal, Bishop of London, well known for his relations with Tyndale. The Bishop had condemned The Scriptures because of dangerous errors of translation. Dr. Barnes questioned his sincerity and submitted as evidence that Bishop Tunstal was doing nothing to make provision for a correct translation. The only conclusion possible, Barnes felt, was that Tunstal did not want the people to have the Bible at all.

Barnes was especially incensed because the Chancellor of London had advised a merchant to buy *Robin Hood* for his servants to read, saying, " What should they do with the Lives of the Fathers or the books of Holy Scripture ? " To another the same Chancellor had said : " What findest thou in the Gospel but a story; what good canst thou take there-out ?" His response to these statements was a fervent prayer :

O Lord God, where art Thou ? Why sleepest Thou ? Why sufferest thou this blasphemy ? Thou hast defended Thy prophets with wild fire from heaven, and wilt Thou suffer Thy only Son and Thy heavenly Word, thus to be despised and to be reckoned but as a story of Robin Hood ? Rise up good Lord. Rise up; Thy enemies do prevail. Thy enemies do multiply; show Thy power, defend Thy glory. It is Thy contumely and not ours. What have we to do with it but alonely to Thy glory. Revenge this cause or Thy enemies shall reckon it not to be Thy cause. O Thou eternal God, though our sins have deserved this, yet look on Thy name, look on Thy verity. See how Thou art mocked. See how Thou art blasphemed, yea, and that by them that have taken on them to defend Thy glory.

But now, heavenly Father, seeing that Thou hast suffered it : yet for the glory of Thy name give some man strength to defend it, or else shalt Thou be clearly taken out of the hearts of all men.

All of Barnes' essays reflect his very great concern for the broad distribution of Scripture among the people because he considered it the only infallible source of religious knowledge and accepted it as the inspired Word of God. His encouragement of the English translators of the Bible at Antwerp and elsewhere is well known. Further, his part in the distribution of Tyndale's Bible during his imprisonment at the Austin friars in London explains Bishop Tunstal's determination to keep him confined. The threat to his life that induced him to flee to the Continent was also the result of his persistence in behalf of the English Bible.

This essay was in the Antwerp edition of Barnes' works. It was not reproduced in the Bydell and Syngleton editions.

10. *That men's constitutions, which are not grounded in Scripture, bind not the conscience of man under pain of deadly sin.*

Less than one fourth of the original has been omitted from this essay as it is reproduced on pages 81 to 93. The whole is a comprehensive exposition of Martin Luther's view of the separate functions of church and state. As such, it was incompatible with the ecclesiastical prerogatives assumed by Henry VIII when he became Defender of the Faith. It was, therefore, not reprinted in the Bydell and Syngleton editions. Its presence in the Antwerp edition may help to explain why the king did not give Barnes an enthusiastic reception when he visited London in December 1531.

Editorial omissions from the original text are chiefly repetitious passages and duplications of illustrative examples. The essay contains very little reference to the bishops and the sins of the religious hierarchy.

11. *That all men are bound to receive the Holy Communion under both kinds under pain of deadly sin.*

This was one of the Lutheran views that Henry VIII most insistently rejected. For that reason its absence in the Bydell and Syngleton editions will occasion no surprise.

Barnes' essay refers to the practice of the ancient church which celebrated communion in both kinds and quotes Christ, St. Paul, and the early church fathers to support his point of view. He suggests that the church either give up its practice of withholding the cup from the layity or deal with Christ and St. Paul as heretics. He attacks the arguments of the church with reference to the jeopardies inherent in giving the cup to laymen and says that, when the Sacrament was instituted, Jesus knew full well that a drop of the cup might be spilled

3

during distribution and also that unworthy men might drink of that cup. He also knew that the body contains blood, yet He did in truth offer both the bread and the wine to the communicants.

A discussion of the question of the real presence is not included in the essay. This did not become an issue in England until after 1531, the date of this essay.

12. *That by God's Word it is Lawful to Priests that hath not the Gift of Chastity, to marry Wives.*

This is much the longest of the essays of Robert Barnes. Strangely it was not in the Antwerp edition of 1531, but was in the later English editions. We can understand why it was not prudent to reprint the essay on civil and ecclesiastical authority, and why the essay on communion in both kinds was not reprinted. The first touched the king's ecclesiastical authority and the second was a doctrine that he was personally desirous of maintaining. But a celibate priesthood was also one of the medieval practices that the king was not willing to abandon. Why then, should an elaborate polemic against it have been published by Barnes in 1534 ?

The essay itself covers familiar ground. The Apostle Paul is extensively quoted and Barnes makes the point that he is not speaking in self-defence because he himself was not married. The most remarkable feature of the essay is the broad knowledge of church history Barnes reveals as well as his thorough acquaintance with the writings of the church fathers. He submits a long list of popes who were the sons of priests and argues cogently for an abolition of the ecclesiastical laws which had made clerical immorality an accepted thing while pious married priests were victims of persecution.

13. *That it is against the Holy Scripture to Honour Images
     and to Pray to Saints.*

The Biblical theology of Robert Barnes is well illustrated
by his essay on images and saints. The viewpoint expressed
was accepted by English theologians during the reign of Henry
VIII with powerful support from Thomas Cromwell.

Rather than beginning by an exhortation on the futility of
honouring images and praying to saints, Barnes' essay intro-
duces the subject by calling attention to the lack of a true
faith in Christ which led to such observances. He says :

> If men had the very true faith in Christ and believed
> that He were God and omnipotent; that if they believed
> that He were merciful, gracious, and loving, and that we
> could desire nothing of Him but He would give it, they
> would go no further but to Him, and they would make,
> devise, and invent no mediators, but faithfully receive Him
> according to Scripture as their only Mediator, Saviour,
> and Redeemer. Also by this faith they should perfectly
> know, that they could not be so unworthy but He of His
> only and mere mercy is able, and also would make them
> worthy to receive their petitions : that they should nor
> ought not to seek any other mediator either to obtain any-
> thing or else to make them worthy, but should know and
> confess both in word and deed that Christ is able enough,
> yea and so mighty and merciful that all other feigned and
> invented mediators of men be vile, filthy, and abominable
> of themselves to be compared to Him.

Relating the honouring of images to the idolatry recorded
in the Old Testament, Barnes pleaded for an obedience to
the First Commandment which forbade the honouring of
graven images, and called for a worship of the true God, and
Him alone.

On the subject of intercession to saints, Barnes quoted St. Paul : " There is one mediator between God and men, the man Christ Jesus ", and closed his argument by saying :

If saints be necessary to be mediators for us, then is Christ insufficient ? And if anything be given us of God for saints' sakes, then be not all things given us for Christ's sake ?

This essay was in the Antwerp edition but not in those of Bydell and Syngleton. This is remarkable in view of the hostile attitude of Henry VIII to the adoration of saints and images.

14. *Of the Original of the Mass.*

This translation of the nineteenth item in Barnes' *Sentences* was included by Foxe in the Daye edition of the works of *Tyndale, Frith, and Barnes.* It traced the historical development of the Mass.

15. *A Collection of Doctors' Testimonies.*

The last section of the Daye edition of Barnes' works is a summary or epitome of all the doctrinal essays. Some of them are translated from *The Sentences.* Others are apparently extracted from essays of Barnes that have been lost.

C. LIVES OF THE POPES

Robert Barnes may well be the first Protestant church historian. It is certain that he was the first to write a history of the papacy. His *Lives of the Popes* was written in Latin and published in 1535 under the title *Vitae Romanorum Pontificum.* Dedicated to Henry VIII, the book was a historical study of the papacy from the beginning to the end of the pontificate of Alexander III in 1181. It was a single volume that included a Latin preface by Martin Luther.

An interesting fragment of Barnes' *Lives* was published both at Wittenberg and at Strassburg in 1545. It described the conflict between Frederick Barbarossa, the Holy Roman Emperor, and Pope Adrian IV and Alexander III. Adrian IV was Nicholas Breakspeare, the only English pope in the history of the papacy. Luther also provided a preface for this publication.

A second edition of the *Lives of the Popes* was published in 1536. The history was brought up to date in a third edition published in 1615. John Bale, Barnes' Cambridge friend, carried the history forward to 1559. John Lydius, a Frankfort theologian, brought it up to the pontificate of Paul V, 1605-1621.

Luther's preface to the first edition closed with the following words :

> Though I was not at first historically well-informed, I attacked the papacy on the basis of Holy Scripture. Now I rejoice heartily to see that others have attacked it from another source, that is from history. I feel that I have triumphed in my point of view as I note how clearly history agrees with Scripture. What I have learned and taught from Paul and Daniel, namely that the Pope is Anti-christ, that history proclaims, pointing to and indicating the very man himself.